MEXICO CITY COLLEGE
The History: 1940 – 1963
and Beyond

By

Joseph M. Quinn

Mayahuel Books
Jed Linde, Editor

Mexico City College
The History: 1940-1963
and Beyond
First Edition, November 1, 2024.
Copyright 2024 by Mayahuel Books.
Written by Joseph M. Quinn.
Edited and expanded by Jed Linde.
Cover: MCC Writing Center's mural;
designed and painted by Norman Bradley,1959.
Cover design: Eric Lang:
Photographs:
Diana by Richard Wilkie
Popocatepetl by Fausto Hernandez
Street Perspective by Gonzalo Servin
A collection of MCC photographs
Covarrubias Mural by Richard Wilkie
Bellas Artes by Bhargava Marripati
Alameda-Mirador by Mikhail Nilov
Mexican 'Spirits' Store by Richard Wilkie
El Angel by Mikhail Nilov
The Arrival – A Fable, first published
in *Uranium Mine and Other Stories*

Table of Contents

Editor's Note

This book contains an expanded *Mexico City College Story: The History 1940-1963.* by Joseph M. Quinn, who published it on a website he created in 2006. It includes the original's text, references, notes, photographs, etc., and much additional material.

The title was changed to include *"and Beyond,"* because after its name change to University of the Americas in 1963, the school continued at the Toluca Highway site until the 1970, when it moved to Puebla. Furthermore, the history itself extends decades after 1963, there are multiple additions to various sections of this book that date after 1963, and there is a new Alumni Memoirs section that includes UA students.

In 2016, getting on in years—as have most MCC alumni—Quinn requested on the MCC Yahoo website (which ended Dec. 2020, when Yahoo closed all groups) that an alumnus take over the website from him, and to fix some glitches in it. After a pause and no candidates, I volunteered. To me, the history he wrote and the supporting materials seemed too valuable to let disappear.

In a series of emails, Joseph guided me through the process of assuming ownership of the website and its contents, including the domain fees. He suggested that I edit the history, with the only caveat being that he remain the author. (I would not have changed that in any case.)

At the time, I had no experience with website administration, maintenance, or repairing. Fortunately, my daughter, Monica, during a visit, reformatted the website and fixed some links, becoming its webmaster.

Recently, I discussed with her who would take over the site from me at some future date, and she suggested, "Why don't you make a book of it?"

I agreed, because a book version would be a functional and enduring copy of the original history website, and allow for multiple additions. The book and future editions could take the place of the website should it become necessary to close it at some future date. Besides, there is an active MCC alumni Facebook group that provides a daily forum.

Having reviewed all the history's materials, I am reminded of how artistically gifted Joseph was, and admire him for all the hard work that went into gathering or composing all the supporting materials and then writing the history and creating the website.

Sadly, Joseph passed on December 29, 2018. His obituary is at the end of this book.

A warm *abrazo* from all of us, Joseph.

-Jed Linde, 2024

Foreword

This project of writing the history of Mexico City College came about because of a lack of related resources, typical being a 70-word paragraph in an early Universidad de las Americas, Puebla publication. The web sites, including the Universidad de las Americas, A.C. one, offered little more. There were many unanswered questions, many regarding the transition from a college into a university.

In 1996 I started contacting alumni, asking questions and researching data. Many, including myself, did not know the difference between the two universities, UDLAP and the UDLA, A.C. They are not related, but both claim Mexico City College as its predecessor. One alumnus in an email asked, "To which institution are we an alumnus?" Over the years, all my correspondence with the UDLA, A.C. institution has gone unanswered; the Puebla institution early correspondence was, at best, evasive, usually referring me back to one of their one-paragraph digests. My "History" probes that reluctance and the academia politics involved.

"The Mexico City College Story: The History 1940-1963" is not a work of scholarship. If it had been, my name would not be attached to it, for among my dwindling pretensions there is no pretense of scholarship. If the shortcomings of this part-time, decade-long project remain within tolerable limits, this is due to the many friends, colleagues, academia and strangers who have permitted me to tax their kindness with inquiries, requests for suggestions, and discussions of doubtful points. If I had more sense and wisdom, I would not have attempted this project.

-Joseph M. Quinn, 2006

Acknowledgements

It is a pleasure to note that this history is, in effect, a product of the spirit of many who were eager to contribute over the years. I thank Dr. Richard W. Wilkie, MCC class of '59, Professor of Geography, University of Massachusetts-Amherst; Professor Edward Simmen, *Docente-Investigador, Deptos. de Lenguas y Literatura, Universidad de las Americas, Puebla (UDLAP);* and Professor Arturo Valentin Arrieta Audiffred, *UDLAP Biblioteca;* for their generous, prompt responses to my many requests for information, photos, and clarification of points. I also thank Terrence Parker, editor of the literary weekly, *The Moon,* for his many excellent suggestions and for proofreading the text.

–Joseph M. Quinn. 2006

As I began the process of transforming the MCC History website into a book, I utilized the alumni Facebook group forum to suggest an alumni section and to request submissions. I thank my fellow alumni for contributing their remarkable memoirs. By chance, at a different alumni website, I came across a picture of Richard Wilkie—now Professor Emeritus of U. of Massachusetts-Amherst—and attempted to contact him. What followed was beyond serendipitous, as Richard became an invaluable resource and Facetime friend. His suggestions and contributions were most helpful, and I offer him many thanks and appreciation for all his assistance.

—Jed Linde, 2024

SaPIENTIA FRaTERNITa
-PAX-Se
MEXICO CITY
COLLEGE 1956-1957
announcement of courses

Mexico City College
The History: 1940 - 1963
By
Joseph M. Quinn

Mexico City College (MCC) was a truly unique institution, where Mexico became part of the school's classroom. Located in the city, and later, the outskirts of the Distrito Federal, it offered a broad liberal arts curriculum ultimately accredited by the Southern Association of Colleges and Schools (SACS). Students and faculty from across the United States and almost three dozen countries, along with a local student body, supported by a multinational faculty, provided an educational environment of extraordinary cultural diversity not matched anywhere else at the time.

Because of embezzlement (more on that later), twenty years after its beginning, it stood on the brink of foundering, and multiple changes took place. Re-named the University of the Américas, it then became the Universidad de las Américas, followed by its move to the city of Puebla, Mexico. Fifteen years later, it divided into two distinct, separate institutions: one still in Puebla, Universidad de las Américas-Puebla (UDLAP), and one back in Mexico City, Universidad de las Américas, A.C. ['Asociación Civil,' designating a nonprofit corporation]."[12]

To appreciate fully the evolution of MCC (later called, "one of the most prestigious private universities in Mexico" [Note M]), its history and politics, requires going back to the opening days of the Second World War. Germany was on the march and U.S. involvement was just a question of time. The large U.S. and English-speaking colony in Mexico City wanted the means to keep their high school grads at home, instead of them heading north for college (and out of parental control), if not impulsive "patriotic enlistment."[2]

Mexico City College (MCC) grew out of one of the great private educational ventures in Latin America — the American School Foundation — and of the aspirations of its superintendent, Dr. Henry L. Cain, and the principal of the High School Department, Dr. Paul V. Murray. Thus, MCC, founded in 1940, was as an extension of the American School Foundation (K-12) with "Sapientia, Pax, Fraternitas" (Wisdom, Peace, Fraternity) chosen as its motto. (Short bios of Dr. Cain and Dr. Murray are at the back of this book.)

Invested as the first president, Dr. Cain served until 1953, when he became President Emeritus. Paul V. Murray served as the first Dean and became President in 1953. Aside from administrative roles, Dr. Cain was the professor of education, and Dr. Murray professor of history.[1] Having lived in Mexico since the late 1930s, Dr. Murray and his wife, Elena Picazo de Murray, published numerous articles and widely adopted text books for language instruction. Later, Murray received an LL.D. from his alma mater, St. Ambrose College.

Dr. Murray, "...articulate and energetic, . . . maintained a close and influential association with the Mexican and foreign business community and with other educational institutions. As the college's official spokesperson, he assumed primary responsibility for maintaining the financial solvency of the College and took justifiable pride in his ability to meet complex payrolls. Since the College enjoys neither diplomatic sponsorship nor immunity, an indispensable prerequisite for its stable functioning is the maintenance of amicable relations with the Government and people of Mexico."[2] "(Murray and Cain) were well-connected within a middle to lower rung of the American-Mexican 'old-boy network.'"[10, Note B,]

Mexico City College opened July 1, 1940 as a junior college in the dining room of a *"casa de huespedes"* (boarding house) at Avenida Tacubaya 40 (currently, Avenida Vasconcelos, 32) with five students, five teachers, five liberal arts courses and Henry L. Cain as President, Paul V. Murray as Dean, and Elizabeth Thomas de Lopez as Registrar. In February, 1941, classes met in the afternoon in the American High School's basement, which later became the large Sears Roebuck store at Avenidas Insurgentes and San Luis Potosi No. 154.

Five years later, the College moved from the American High School to Calle San Luis Potosi 131, and eventually occupied various office buildings and apartment houses along of Chiapas, San Luis Potosi, and Zacatecas streets. Elizabeth Lopez became the first full-time MCC employee.[9]

In the first commencement exercises June 27, 1944, twelve graduates received diplomas as Associates in Arts and Sciences. This "degree," no longer awarded, represented four years of work, but not within a recognized college curriculum, which MCC had yet to offer.[1] Receiving Associate in Arts diplomas were Helen Scott Gilland, Mary Gilland, Pepita Garcia Colin, Mary Gisholt, Thomas Koralek, Fernando Peñalosa, Leonore Ross, and William Valverde. Those who received the Associate in Science diploma were Guillermo

Ahumada, Elaine Rosslyn Gladston, Gilbert Haakh and Lavern A. Miller. Guillermo Ahumada was the valedictorian. Nine of the ten members of the faculty were present: Henry Cain, Paul Murray, Albert Bork, Brita Bowen, José Gaos, Atlanta Cole, Montes de Oca, Dimitri Sokoloff, Jesse Vera, and Bonita Clark Wrixton .A

In January, 1946 a group of nine students arrived from Ohio State University for the first Winter Quarter in Mexico (WQIM) program. A month later the Veterans Administration placed MCC on the list of schools approved for study under the G.I. Bill of Rights.[1] Three American veterans of World War II enrolled. Student enrollment was now 75.[9]

Students often lived upstairs or next door to the building that housed their classrooms. The Student ID Card provided free access to the Hacienda Club, with its tennis courts, basketball and handball courts, a swimming pool and steam baths. The Club was located seven blocks from the San Luis Potosi campus.

In the next twelve years more than six thousand north-of-the-border students attended MCC.

Like the student body, the early faculty during the late 1940s and '50s represented over ten nationalities,[21] including England, France, Germany, Italy, Portugal and Spain, personifying and symbolizing the democratic values of cultural diversity and tolerance. Many of the faculty migrated to Mexico from Europe following the Spanish Civil War and, later, World War II. A majority were western Europeans – among them José Gaos, co-chairman of graduate studies, who was formerly the rector of the University of Madrid and professor of History and Anthropology, and Pedro Bosch Gimpera, former rector of the University of Barcelona and former Catalonian Minister of the Interior. The former Czechoslovakian Minister to Mexico, Vaclav Laska, taught history and government. Baron Alexander von Wuthenau, from Germany, who was a cousin of the British royal family, taught the history of art, and assisted the Mexican government in the restoration of its colonial art treasures.[1,2]

MCC's connection with the American School Foundation ended in June, 1946, when the ASF sold the high school building to Sears Roebuck and ASF moved to its new campus in *Colonia Tacubaya*.[9]

Dr. Henry Cain and Paul Murray, co-founders and co-owners of MCC, legally changed the status of the school from a proprietary institution to an Asociación Civil, in July 31, 1950. This paved the way for acceptance by the Texas Association of Colleges as an overseas institution and, later (December 2, 1959), membership in the Southern Association of Colleges and Schools (SACS).

Elena Picazo de Murray, assisted by Donlon Havenes, formed the department of English for Mexicans in January, 1951, in its own building at Calle Jalapa 148, across the street from the MCC Art Center. Within two years 1,300 students enrolled in the day and evening classes that offered thirteen courses in English proficiency,[1] with thirty classes and twenty-three instructors. The Center also provided club activities and social programs. Her Spanish text book, *Everyday Spanish: An Idiomatic Approach*, regarded as one of the best in the field, was used by countless American students at MCC, and adopted by several U.S. colleges and universities.

By May, 1951, the MCC campus consisted of seven buildings in Colonia Roma, spread over an area of six blocks: three of the latest additions being at Calle San Luis Potosi 132 and 136, and one on the corner of Tonela and Chiapas. The post office address for the College was Calle San Luis Potosi 135.

Some of these émigrés, many artists, writers and intelligentsia, were expatriates from the cold-war era and the United States Congress' investigation of the U.S. film industry for alleged 'un-American' activities. To make ends meet, some of these political and cultural expatriates, both from the U.S. and Europe, turned to teaching at MCC, The National University of Mexico, and the American School Foundation. (K–12)[16]

MCC Professor Dr. Miguel Barrios taught spoken and written Nahuatl and, working with a group of graduate anthropology students, compiled the only grammar-dictionary of the Nahuatl language, still spoken by two million Indians in many areas of Mexico.[1] Later, professor Fernando Horcasitas would expand upon this dictionary. [Note C] MCC was the only institution in the world offering classes in spoken Maya and Nahuatl. On May 12, 1950, Dr. Barrios started publishing the *Mexihkatl Itonalma*. This small newspaper, written only in Nahuatl for the non-Spanish speaking Indians, was the only literature available to this language group, and those who wanted to learn to write and read in their language. The work of Drs. Barrios and Horcasitas and their students resulted in the preservation of much of Nahuatl and Mayan oral folk history. (*The Collegian*, May 19, 1950)

Robert Weitlaner, Mexico's foremost ethnologist, served as Associate Professor of Anthropology. He was also director of the government's National Institute of Anthropology, and regarded as the foremost ethnologist in Mexico. He made the reconstruction of Indian dialects and cultures his life's work. Flora Botton taught Philosophy; she was the only surviving member of her family of ten from the Nazi death camps. Her philosophy classes included European history and first-hand accounts of the camps. During the late 1940s and early '50s there were a handful of students and instructors at MCC who related their personal stories of keeping one step ahead of the Nazis as they made their way across Western Europe to Spain and safety. Dr. Paul G. Fried, the Chief Translator for the Nuremburg War Crime Trials, taught history. Dr. Richard E. Greenleaf, Professor of History and International Relations, was a recognized international expert in reading sixteen-century Spanish paleography. Dr. Silvio Zavala, Director of the Nacional Museo de Historia, taught history at MCC.

Dr. Pablo Martínez del Río was one of the more colorful professors on campus. Director of the Escuela Nacional de Antropología e Historia de la Universidad Nacional, president and chairman of many boards and societies, including president of the Board of Directors of the Benjamin Franklin Library (U.S. Embassy), Manager of the Alameda Branch of the Banco Nacional de México, member of the French Legion of Honor, member of the Board of Trustees of MCC, to name a few, he had represented Mexico in many educational and scholarly congresses both at home and abroad. But the students of MCC best remember him for his crisp Oxford accent, immaculate dress with homburg, spats, and umbrella-cane, accented by a brisk stride. His classes in History and Anthropology were always full. This was a man who lived the history he taught, having once rode as a young man with Pancho Villa.

In the summer of 1946, Dr. James B. Tharp, education professor at Ohio State University (as mentioned earlier), pioneered the "Summer Quarter in Mexico" program (WQIM), which soon included the winter quarter. Initially, nine co-eds attended. By the mid-fifties, an average of 180 students participated in the WQIM program. This program spread to other schools, including

Michigan State University, Notre Dame, Georgetown University School of Foreign Service, University of Arizona, Vanderbilt and Peabody Teachers College in Nashville, and others. Not only students, but teachers from the U.S. and Canada attended one of the two summer Workshops in Latin American Cultures. This annual five-week session offered extensive work in the Spanish language and in Mexican social studies and crafts.[1]

During the late 1940s and early '50s, the MCC campus was the subject of numerous articles in magazines, newspapers and Sunday supplements motivated, no doubt, by the uniqueness of the institution, the interest shown by veterans, and the "Quarter in Mexico" (WQIM) program. The print media in the U.S. would refer to MCC as the "gringo campus below the border." A 1958 Mexican map of Mexico City listed it among the "puntos de interes," the "Colegio Americano."

In 1946, MCC became a 4-year college conferring the BA degree. The MCC graduate school — "Centro de Estudios Universitarios" — opened in September, 1947 with Drs. Lorna L. Stafford and Jose Gaos as co-directors. Master of Arts degrees were offered in Anthropology, Business Administration (Foreign Trade), Creative Writing, Economics, History, International Relations, and Spanish. The Graduate School also included the Master of Fine Arts degree.[21] In ten years, a total of 2,800 graduate students entered the program with 72 admitted to major institutions in the U.S., England, France, Sweden, Spain, Switzerland, and Mexico for doctoral studies. Of these, fifteen are faculty with U.S. universities (1957). Joseph H. Matluck was the first MCC graduate awarded a *Doctor en Letras*, from the *Universidad Nacional*, 1951.

Jimenez Moreno and Pedro Bosch Gimpera founded the Department of Anthropology in 1946. The following year, twenty-one students received four-year undergraduate degrees. The total for the 1951-52 academic year was 175 B.A.s and 61 M.A.s. By June, 1957, the College had awarded 1,113 Bachelor of Arts degrees and 273 Master's degrees.[1,2]

On July 2, 1947 the first college newspaper, *El Conquistador de Mexico City College* came out, but the (ill-conceived) title lasted only nineteen issues. Between April and July, 1948, the paper became *El Grito de Mexico City College* (from Father Hidalgo's "Grito de Dolores" call for Mexican independence). By fall 1948, the newspaper again changed its name, this time to *The Mexico City*

Collegian. The early issues featured, to the left of the title, an American eagle holding a U.S. shield, and to the right of the title, a Mexican eagle clasping a snake with its talons and beak. Between December, 1950 and April 12, 1951, the subtitle "The Official Publication of Mexico City College" appeared.

Dean Murray contributed an article in almost every issue of the campus newspaper. First, the column was titled "From the Dean's Desk" and, when he became President, "From the President's Desk."

One alumnus remembers Dr. Paul Murray as wearing "his religion on his sleeve" and was, to some, "familiarly known as 'Pious Paul.'" Murray, in his column "From the Dean's Desk," (*The Collegian*, August 15, 1949), although he praised the acting of the MCC students, was quick to express his conservatism and religious values when he wrote that the recent four one-act Tennessee Williams plays, presented by MCC Studio Players, was "vacuous drivel . . .. Is this the best offering from modern playwriting . . . where 'God' has been reduced to 'god' and 'damn' to 'dam?'"

Starting with the January 28, 1954 issue, the *Collegian* added a new subtitle, "The American College South of The Border."This subtitle remained and prompted the 1961 outgoing editor John Revett to tell the new editor Doug Butterworth, "At one time this little slogan probably had its place, but today it's simply not enough." To make his point, he satirically suggested there be a Mexican institution in the U.S. with the following slogan, "*Universidad Mexicana Norte de la Frontera.*"20 ("MCC Moves with Changing World")

The College academic philosophy was spelled out in the 1957-58 College catalogue: "The administrators of Mexico City College believe that a broad liberal arts program is the best basis for general education...History, literature, philosophy, logic, ethics, art, music, geography, English and Spanish form the basis of cultural orientation at the college." [21]

In 1961, *The MCC Collegian* was honored for the fourteenth consecutive year with the "All American Honor" rating by the Associated Collegiate Press: the highest obtainable by a college newspaper (*The Collegian,* May 26, 1961). Brita Bowen was the advisor to *The Collegian,* as well as Director of Public Relations. For the first time, a short-lived column in Spanish, "Sección Española" appeared in the July 30, 1959 issue.

Peter and Lucia Montague published a short-lived alternative school paper, called *"The Gadfly"* (more on this later) in 1961. There were only four issues, the last in December, 1961.[13, Note I]

The MCC football team, the "Aztecas," was formed in 1947 and admitted to the most important American football conference in Mexico, the Liga Mayor. Much of the financial support for the team came personally from Paul Murray. Of the local promoters, only "Dr. Murray had a credit card which they could use to bring a selected team down for the annual Aztec Bowl game." In 1949 the Aztecas won its first championship: the final match of that season was against the Pumas Dorados de la UNAM.[4, See Note L for a history of football at MCC]

Sports at MCC usually commanded a full page in *The Collegian*, occasionally two pages (titled "The Collegian Sports Parade"), [Note L] and fencing was always a part of MCC sports. In March, 1953, the Latin American Fencing Society of MCC was invited to become a member of the *Associación de Esgrima del Distrito Federal en Funciones de Federación*. This organization is the most distinguished fencing association in Mexico, and its membership included the best fencers in the country. The Fencing Club has been under the leadership of Cambridge educated Spaniard Carlos M. Sagasta, MCC professor of Ancient History and Fencing Mastery.

"The one thing that impresses me about Mexico City College," says Sagasta, "is the fact that students seem to be here to study, not to play." (*The MCC Collegian*, November 26, 1952)

MCC excelled in courses of International Relations and Latin American studies, Art, Creative Writing and Journalism. The campus was the only center in Latin America providing higher studies for the American student intent in Business Administration and Foreign Trade in Latin America.[21]

The Art Department opened in January, 1947 with six students at Calle San Luis Potosi 154, when Merle Wachter was the only art teacher. (Prior to this inauguration, Manuel Aguirre, the head librarian at the American School, served as the MCC Art Education instructor.) In 1951, the Art Department, with the addition of sculpture Professor German Cueto, and a student enrollment of 200, became the sole occupant of the building at 132 San Luis Potosi, on the corner of Insurgentes and Coahuila. Justino Fernandez, a leading Orozco authority, also taught in the art department. When the College moved to Km. 16, Professor Wachter headed an international staff of twelve professors and instructors, each specializing in some area of the fine arts. Arnold Belkin taught mural techniques and art history, and painted many murals throughout Mexico. Many established artists have listed studying at Mexico City College, either for one quarter or for several years, in their bios. Some would alternate in attending schools between MCC and the San Miguel de Allende Art Institute and Allende's Escuela Universitaria de Bellas Artes.[17] Stage Design started in the Summer Quarter, 1956, when Richard Posner became. Director of the Studio Stages

Merle Wachter received an honorary doctorate from the University in June, 1969. This was in recognition of his work not only at MCC, but within the greater Mexican community. On September of the same year, Dr. Wachter took the position of Dean of the Graduate School, succeeding Dr. Richard Greenleaf.

The Mexico City Writing Center, the first of its kind in Latin America and a branch of MCC, was founded in the summer of 1950 by Margaret Shedd, a California novelist (who in private life was Mrs. Oliver Kissick). The Center was located at Chiapas 136. "About fifty student writers (from the U.S. and Mexico) have enrolled in each quarterly session."[1] Two years after its founding Miss Shedd initiated a joint project of the Center and the Rockefeller Foundation's Division of the Humanities and Social Sciences. The Project awarded five scholarships, worth $1500 apiece, to young Mexican writers. The scholarships entitled their holders to two terms of study in the Writing Center. Seventy-five candidates applied for the initial scholarships, and the Rockefeller Foundation indicated its willingness to continue the program for the young Mexican writers "over a period of three years, perhaps longer." Miss Shedd believed "that the young (MCC) students at the Center will richly benefit from their association with their gifted Mexican colleagues."[18]

The Center was next headed by Ted Robbins and Jerry Moss Olson, both published authors, with an international staff that included James Norman

Schmidt and the Spanish-Mexican philosopher Ramón Xirau. A unique feature of the Creative Writing department was the "Creative Two-Way Spanish-English Translation" class, supervised by Ramon Xirau and editor and author Donald Demarest of New York (*The Dark Virgin: The Book of Our Lady of Guadalupe*), emphasizing the two-way translation of things and images from one language to another.[1]

In December, 1950, the Writing Center, working with the MCC Studio Stages drama students under the direction of Earl Sennett, started bi-weekly radio shows on Station XEBS, with half-hour dramatic presentations.

Norman Mailer, Vance Bourjaily and John Steinbeck lectured at the College, along with "Mexican playwright Rodolfo Usigli; Leopoldo Zea of the School of Philosophy and Letters of Mexico's National University; José Luis Martinez, author of Mexican *Literature of the Twentieth Century;* José García Ascot, poet, editor and translator; and Señora Maria de Leon Ortega, authority on Latin American folk music."[7,18] The "beat" generation icon and author, Jack Kerouac, briefly attended MCC.[10]

Theatre was always a part of MCC. Dr. Helene Gaubert was the first to establish a Drama Workshop in the early 40s, assisted later by Rick Brown and Sandra Stewart.

Earl Sennett, English and Drama instructor, was the founder and guiding light of the Studio Players, which made its debut in August, 1949, when it staged the four Tennessee Williams one-act plays (that drew critical comments from Dean Murray) at the Bugambilia Club. Ed Torrence, protégé of the famous New York director Margo Jones, directed the one-act plays, with the staging theatre-in-the-round, a first for Mexico. It was Glen Hughes of the University of Washington and Ms. Jones who separately developed this intimate form of theatre. Sennett was also the director for the English colony Mexico City Players. When Sennett left for New York in 1954, the Studio Players remained dormant until Dave Roberts, the new Speech and Drama instructor, revived the group.

Richard Posner became director of Studio Stages in April, 1956. His first production with Studio Stages was Miller's *A View from A Bridge,* presented in May, 1956. Five years later, the February 15, 1961 *MCC Collegian* wrote that *The View* "is still generally considered to be one of the best English-language productions ever given in the city." Posner founded the Fine Arts Committee in 1960 to stimulate interest in theatre activities at MCC. He believed that the Studio Stage was potentially important for the MCC writing and art students, and established close cooperation between the Art Department (which offered a course in stage design), the library (which expanded its works on dramatic scripts), and the Writing Center (which encouraged its students to write scripts for the MCC dramatic group).

Posner, a New Yorker, joined the English Department in the summer of 1955 as a visiting professor teaching Writing for TV, and has been a special lecturer in the Writing Center. He directed his first production in Mexico, Thornton Wilder's *The Skin of Our Teeth*, for the English-speaking colony's Players, A.C. Organized in 1951, this off-campus group was and is the oldest of four major drama groups in Mexico devoted to English-speaking plays.

A member of Elia Kazan's and Lee Strasberg's Actor's Studio, Posner was also a member of the New Dramatists (a playwright's workshop), an associate editor of the *United Nations World,* and a New York theatre reporter for *Billboard* magazine. He had written numerous short stories and dramatic scripts, which had earned him his appointment to the select New Dramatists group.

Jack Natkin founded the MCC literary group, the *Poet's Voice* readers' theatre, during the 1959 Fall quarter. The group's first productions were two dramatic readings: "The Microscopic Morality," and "The Ants."

The late Professor William L. Sherman, University of Nebraska-Lincoln, a '59 MCC graduate in History, co-authored (along with Meyer) *The Course of Mexican History*, still advertised as "the leading text book on Mexican history from the pre-Columbian periods to the present." It is now in its seventh edition.

"Mesoamerican Notes" No. 1, published in 1950, was founded by Robert Barlow who chaired the Department of Anthropology in 1949. Barlow printed 350 copies of the first edition on a hand press in his home. It was trilingual (Náhuatl, Spanish, and English) and included articles by Miguel Barrios, Frederick A. Peterson (who published, later, *Ancient Mexico*), and Professor Fernando Horcasitas. Professor Robert Barlow (1918-1951), anthropologist, also taught classical Nahuatl at the *Escuela Nacional de Antropología*. Note C

Numerous scholars, most from the U.S., used MCC as a base to pursue their field studies in pre-Columbian history, study and research. It was the abundance of Mexico's untapped pre-Columbian sites that gave MCC its reputation as a major center for pre-Columbian history, study and research in anthropological and archeological field studies. The MCC archaeological department was credited with the discovery and development of many archaeological sites.

"In 1956, scholarly articles by members of the faculty were collected in a thick, bilingual volume, entitled *Antología MCC 1956*, which the College presented as a contribution to the Seventh Mexican Book Fair (Feria del Libro)."[2] A year later, MCC opened the Oaxaca Archaeological Research Center *(Centro de Estudios Regionales)*. MCC professors and students were instrumental in many archaeological discoveries, including the Yagul site near Oaxaca.

The Texas Association of Colleges accepted the university as an overseas institution in 1951. Eight years later, on December 2, 1959, MCC received full membership in the Southern Association of Colleges and Schools (SACS).

In March, 1954, the college moved to 20 acres of land at Km. 16.5, Carretera Mexico-Toluca (Highway 15) and started expanding the existing physical buildings of what had been the Turf Country Club. Spring classes started April 16, 1954, five months after the start of negotiations to buy this property. The "Toluca Highway" is the continuation of the Paseo de la Reforma.

The Turf Club was founded in 1946 by Axel Faber, a Danish businessman. Land had been sold around the Club for residences for those who wanted to live near the Club. In 1954, MCC purchased the remaining 80,000 square meters along with the principal buildings (from Posada Mimosa Co., owner of the property). This area, situated on a prominence above the Valley of Mexico, has been witness to the birth and growth of Mexico. (See Note J)

The small villages of Cuajimalpa, adjoining Contadero, and "out in the wilds" of Acopilco, were just two miles up the highway from the new campus, separated from the college by fields and small farms. Contadero, described as "a quiet little Mexican village," was the home of the Dean of Admissions and Registrar, Elizabeth Thomas de Lopez. Overlooking Mexico City, these villages would also become a haven for adventurous (if not the beatnik and bohemian fringe) students on limited budgets and seeking a bucolic life style. These students represented a minority of approximately a dozen and half students (less than 2 tenths of one percent of the total average late '50s population). A few students lived adjacent to the campus in six- and eight-unit apartment houses on Avenida de los Volcanes, known as the "lower road," beneath the campus. These units were originally built when the campus was the Turf Country Club. In 1956, there were twenty-seven family groups, either married couples or brothers and sisters, attending MCC as students.

The majority of students either rented apartments or lived with a Mexican or American family in the metropolis. There were no dormitories at MCC. "Most students living in Mexico City caught the MCC school bus — the "Toluca Rocket" — behind the fountain of Diana, the Huntress, located in the center of the circular *glorieta* where their broad avenue *Paseo de la Reforma* angles west and Chapultepec Park begins."[16] The MCC bus departed every half hour to make the ten-mile trip up to the Campus.

Financially, MCC survived into the mid-late 1950s without worthy endowment, without government subsidy, and with little foundation support: It was almost wholly dependent upon tuition payments.[2] "Dean Murray even mortgaged his home to support the school at one point. "[Note B] In Summer, 1960, MCC received its first grant from the National Science Foundation providing scholarships for 10 students of archaeology to study at MCC.[9, Note K]

It was the large veteran enrollment after WW II and the Korean War, and the progressive exodus of veterans and students from U.S. college campuses to one or more semesters of serious study at MCC that gave the college the financial stability and growth it needed. A double-page spread on MCC and the new Korean Bill of Rights appeared in the September 8, 1952 issue of the *Pacific Stars and Stripes* (the official Army daily at Tokyo, Japan for the U.S. Forces in the Far East Command). Within weeks the Registrar's office was swamped by a deluge of letters and applications for admission.

By the end of 1946, WW II veterans constituted 33.5 percent of all 160 students, and by 1950 they comprised 69 percent of the 800-odd students. By the Fall of 1956, veterans had dropped to 56 percent. The veteran enrollment slowly declined thereafter, but the total enrollment remained high.[2] A U.S. official from the Visa Department of the U.S. Embassy would arrive at the college to distribute $115 VA checks to the Vets.

The tuition fee in 1957-58, which included a $10 medical fee, was $130 per quarter, up from $105 two years earlier.[16]

One complaint during the '50s was that "faculty salaries are deplorably low." One of "the highest paid" faculty members in 1956, a Political Science Professor, received "$240 – and later, $260 – per month." "Competent members of the faculty have remained only because they are willing to make material sacrifices in order to live in or carry on research in Mexico."[2]

Mexico, in the 40s and 50s, had much to offer. Crawford Kilian summed it up when he wrote, "We could walk through the ruins of conquered empires, learn the subtleties of bullfighting, and begin to speak the language. Mexican food had substance and flavor, and light and color were more intense. . .. The streets and markets were so beautiful, the people so vivid, the sun so bright, and the air so clear that it seems impossibly romantic," as quoted by Mexico City writer Diana Anhalt in her "Bridging the Cultural Gap".

By 1956, of all Americans enrolled in schools of higher education outside the US, "more (911) attended MCC than any other institution in the world. Besides Mexican and United States nationals, 69 students representing 37 countries were in residence during the summer of 1957."[2] One-hundred fifty-eight colleges and universities were represented on the MCC campus during the summer of 1960. The international student body of MCC, with its heterogeneous intellectual composition, did not resemble the student body of a small American college.

Because of the international composition of the student body and teachers, there were also a "small group of 'cold-war agents' (CIA, FBI, KGB) pretending to be students," checking out the social and political lives of students and faculty, and the cold-war repatriates and international refugees.[16, 19]

MCC history professor Robert L. Bidwell wrote, "There are few places in the New World in which one is so constantly reminded of the roll of centuries, of the unknown peoples who preceded him, and of the tapestry of cultures about him . . . the juxtaposition of cultures and ages . . . as in this Valley of Mexico." (*The Collegian*, October 30, 1958) [Note J]

Mexico became part of the school's classroom. Mexico City in the 1950s has been compared to the Paris of the 20s "where ideas, art, literature and revolution could be discussed" on and off campus, in the classrooms, the sidewalk cafés, and the all-night parties. Life along the Paseo de la Reforma was compared with the Champs Elysees.[16] Some of the Bohemian scenes of Paris for the movie, Hemingway's *The Sun Also Rises*, were shot in the old quarters of Mexico City in 1956. A few MCC students served as extras, not only in this movie but other American and, when a "gringo" was needed, in Mexican movies. [16]

Several MCC students studied bullfighting at the Rancho del Charro, and performed in the Arena. Most notably was Kansas City student John Patrick Jacobs who received his "Ole's."

Maria Elena ("Elenita") Quijada, bursar for MCC and teacher of Spanish, reflected in the February 16, 1961 issue of *The Collegian,* "We had some unusual students. One we still talk about is the fellow who walked around campus with one gold earring in his ear and a parrot on his shoulder."

This was 1953, the year before the college moved to Km. 16. He was still on campus after the move to the new campus, which prompted one alumnus to write, "MCC was the first place I had ever seen a guy in a robe, beard and Jesus sandals with a parrot on his shoulder. Better than anything Berkeley ever dreamed of, even with Ginsberg and Mario Savio sneaking around." Another alumnus speculated that the parrot, sitting on his shoulder next to his ear, fed him the answers during exam week.

The Explorer's Club offered students the opportunity to discover remote vistas of Mexico one would never have expected to exist, much less to visit. Bill Stewart was the founder (1955) of the Explorer's Club, and Brita Bowen was the academic advisor. Between quarters or on weekends, students climbed Popocatépetl or forded rivers on "roadless" roads. Many students, on their own or through the Explorer's Club, would travel throughout Mexico, and some south to Guatemala before there was a road connecting the two countries, into the Yucatán Peninsula, accessible in the '50s by rail only, ("Cancun" was an unnamed isolated beach), and into the many villages accessible only by trail or river boat. In 1954, students Craig and Shirley (last name not recorded) rode their bicycles (via bus and boat, where necessary) from Mexico City to Mérida, in the Yucatán Peninsula. In 1956 six Explorer's Club students embarked on a six-month expedition along the 500-mile course of the Coroni River in Venezuela, into a vast, relatively unexplored jungle.

Indeed, education for the MCC student in Mexico extended far beyond the campus for those whose minds were receptive. [See 16] The three key administrators were President Murray, Vice-President and Dean of Faculty John V. Elmendorf, and Dean of Admissions and Registrar Elizabeth Thomas de Lopez. Their "commitment, both professionally and vocationally, are total." Dean Elmendorf, Ph.D. from the University of North Carolina had a background as professor of Linguistics. Mrs. Lopez (M.A., St. Louis University), was the first full-time staff member, hired in 1947.[2]

Since 1950 the College was chartered under the laws of Mexico as a nonprofit corporation, Associación Civil, or A.C. The early '50s growth was such that in September, 1956, Drs. Cain and Murray established a distinguished Board of Trustees of local American business leaders and a few Mexicans (along with a 10-member Honorary Board of Advisors mostly of US based academia).[2] In effect, this move eventually took absolute control out of Drs. Murray and Cain's hands (and, ironically, eventually led to President Murray ousted by this very Board).

Members of this Board included Drs. Cain and Murray; Lic. Germán Fernández del Castillo, legal counsel of the College; Dr. Pablo Martínez del Río, Director of *Escuela National de Antropológia e Historia* and a noted Mexican scholar; Fraine B. Rhuberry, General Manager of the Ford Motor Company in Mexico; and William B. Richardson, first Board Chairman, and retired executive Vice-President of the National City Bank of New York and former manager of the Bank's branch in Mexico.[2, Notes G & H]

Prompted in part by the necessity for full U.S. academic accreditation and to take advantage of available U.S. foundation and governmental funding, the college moved to non-profit status and formed a Board of Trustees. Veteran enrollment had dropped to less than half by 1957, but enrollment remained high, "suggesting that a student body of viable size can be maintained in the face of declining veteran enrollment. As the percentage of veterans dropped, the proportion of women in the student body had risen. A more 'traditional' and 'feminine' student body also has meant a more stable, less transient, student population. Whereas full-time students accounted for only about 55 per cent of the summer quarter enrollment in 1950, they comprised 85 per cent during the summer of 1957."[2]

Senator Wayne Morse, Democrat from Oregon, was the guest speaker at the fifteenth MCC commencement on June 11, 1959. The Senator has shown a keen interest in Latin American affairs and in MCC and the work the College was doing in Latin American Studies.

The College was changing, foreshadowed no doubt by inconsequential events that began to appear between 1959–1961: the offhand questioning of the relevance of the slogan, "The American College South of the Border," the introduction of a *Sección Española* column in *The Collegian (May 13, 1959)*, the decreasing enrollment of Americans (especially Vets) countered by an increase in Mexican enrollment, and the short-lived publication of the alternate (underground) student newspaper, *The Gadfly.* [Note I]

The fifties ended with a lingering, growing reputation that MCC was a college of bearded, sandaled (if not barefooted) pot-smoking beatniks (with some faculty included), publicized, no doubt, by an early '50s incident involving several MCC students with William Burroughs and the death of his wife. At the time, "a sizable number of (the Veterans) were less interested in their studies than in wild parties and nightlife."[10, Note B, pp. 17,42; Note I] This "reputation," magnified by an insignificant few, is far from the large number of '50s and early '60s graduates who have gone on to establish themselves as successful leaders in their chosen field, both in business and academia. Professor Richard Wilkie notes, "Throughout the US, there are at least 25 to 30 professors, or more, most with doctorates, who have been students at MCC during the high-water years of that institution between 1954-1962. For a small college, that is an impressive record."[16]

The sixties opened with tempestuous winds that endangered the college: In 1960, the loss of much of the College financial reserves through embezzlement; in 1961, William Richardson, Chair of the MCC Board of Trustees forcibly deposed (some say, an action that came too late); and, in 1962, President Dr. Paul V. Murray forced into retirement.

Financial disaster struck on January 27, 1961 when the college learned that its business manager-treasurer, Juan Hernández Avila, born in Texas and a Mexican citizen, (hired in the summer, 1951) absconded with college funds ($100,000 to $250,000, depending upon the source). Hernández was Found in Washington State on February 10, 1961 (13 days after flying to Los Angeles from Mexico City), while trying to cross into Canada, minus the money, and sent back to Mexico. Not prosecuted, he promised to sell his home in Cuernavaca and repay MCC, but later "reneged."[4] The school, "as a privately financed venture," was now "$497,000.00 in debt and on the brink of scuttling."[5,7,9]

"On January 29, 1961, MCC officials met at the home of Board Chairman William Richardson to discuss the seriousness of the problem created by Hernández, and explored the possibility of closing the school. The co-founder and former President Dr. Henry L. Cain, who had retired June 11, 1953, became the Acting Business Manager along with William E. Rogers as Assistant Business Manager. On February 18, Gorden Sweet, Executive Secretary of the Southern Association of Colleges and Schools (SACS) visited the campus to discuss the grave situation created by Hernández. According to Dr. Paul Murray, Sweet suggested to him that he resign."[9]

Dr. Paul V. Murray retired as president of MCC, effective May 1, 1961.[Note F]

The Board of Trustees established a Committee on Internal Reorganization, and the Mexico City College Administrative Council (L.L. Stafford, Elizabeth López, Mildred Allen, and María Elena Quijada.[9]), upon Dr. Murray's resignation, acted as collective president of the college until the Board of Trustees named a new president. Six subcommittees formed to study Mexico City College problems.[20] ("Committees Proposed Changes to Trustees.")

William Richardson resigned as Board President, May 29, 1961. At the time, one individual noted to the President of Tuffs University, "Mexico City College had made its greatest stride forward in years by forcibly deposing Bill Richardson from the board of trustees. The general feeling, however, is that the action came too late and that Richardson's leadership has been so misdirected and yet so strong that the college will probably go under in the next year or so." Note H

Two months later (July 22), the school appointed Dr. Henry L. Cain as interim-president. In December, Dr. Cain and Russell Moody (William Richardson's replacement as Board of Trustees president) attended a SACS meeting where Gorden Sweet introduced Dr. Ray Lindley, president of Texas Christian University. In January, the college invited Dr. Lindley "to 'name his price' to become president of MCC."[9]

Dr. Ray Lindley, a "tall, iron haired"[7] clergyman, took office as the third president of MCC on July 16, 1962. Dr. Jacinto Quidarte became the Dean of Men, replacing Vice President and Dean of Faculty John V. Elmendorf who had earlier moved on (January, 1961) to Brown University (Providence, RI) as Vice President. Dr. Richard Greenleaf became MCC's Academic Vice-President.

With a broom in one hand, administrative academic credentials in the other, and a "revivalist" attitude, Dr. Lindley set out to (1) rid "the institution of the stigma of being a college of beatniks;" (2) to raise the student proportion of non-Americans to 50 percent; and (3) change the Board of Trustees to have no more than half the trustees Americans and the remainder Mexicans, and "with the staff also divided 50-50 between US and other countries." *[Author's note: Was this the premature birth of Affirmative Action?]*

Lindley prohibited beards and barefoot sandals. There was one infamous casualty to Dr. Lindley's reforms: "a student who duly shaved his beard but refused to put on shoes."[5, 13] As recalled by an on-the-spot MCC alumnus, "The casualty was (a student) who had his feet/sandals inspected by Jacinto Quirarte, Dean of Men, who then gave him a note pronouncing that he had permission to wear huaraches. This famous 'Foot Sniffing Certificate,' promptly posted on the school's main bulletin board and discovered by one of the administrators, caused the student's expulsion on the spot." He finished his degree at Kent State in Ohio.[6,13, Note I]

The consequences of Dr. Lindley's reforms eventually resulted in transforming what was until now an American college for Americans in Mexico, into a Mexican college in Mexico for Mexicans. By then most of the VA students were gone and a new source of student population was appearing. His campaign was successful: Mexican student enrollment jumped from 117 in 1962-63 to 425 in 1963-64, slowly filling the gap left by the vanishing Veterans.[5]

The extraordinary MCC era had ended. Within a decade and half, the MCC philosophy of a true liberal arts education had completely disappeared.

(For a summary of how President Macias Rendon (1975-76) changed UDLAP from a liberal arts institution into a technocratic institution to provide job training for engineers, and the decade long battle to reverse the trend, see 16).

On March 19, 1963 Dr. Lindley and the Board of Trustees changed the name from Mexico City College to the University of the Américas, with the school officially achieving university status the same year. The new president managed "to reduce the debt from $550K to a (manageable) $180K." By July, 1964, the school's debt eliminated, the college burned the outstanding note at a special on-campus luncheon.[9] Plans were announced for a ten-million-dollar fund raising campaign.[5]

A new university seal, approved in July, 1965, consisted of a jaguar and eagle and the Latin Motto, "Americanarum Universitas," meaning American women's university. Class rings with this error continued in use until 1970. The mistake discovered, the official seal changed to read "Americarum Universitas," and new class rings ordered,.[9]

However, there was predictable resentment to Dr. Lindley's sweeping changes by some long-term students, some faculty (some resigned), and a few American trustees. "The focus of most resentment is . . . Dr. Ray Lindley,"[7] accumulating in "a series of protests published by students (in) 'The Gadfly,' a very irreverent newspaper which publicized the 'foot-sniffing expulsion,' ridiculed Dr. Lindley's reforms, and poked fun at some of the actions and some individuals in the Mexican government." [6, Note I]

MCC campus had always attracted unique, free spirited, adventurous individuals, both in its faculty and student body. Dr. Denton Ray Lindley, who served as President until 1971, was a former clergyman with an extensive Southern religious background, who had served as educational administrator in various religious schools in the South. One former MCC student described the campus as "always moving, always searching." The type of student and faculty population President Lindley sought would not function well – even on a short-term basis – as "expatriates." The value of the expatriate ambiance as an asset may have escaped Dr. Lindley, or his conservative approach determined his actions. Regardless, the school's atmosphere of adventurous freedom slowly changed under his tutelage.

Early in the 1960s, a search began for a new University campus. The reason for this is not known. (Possibly, with the '68 Olympics on the horizon, the appreciation for the Carretera Mexico-Toluca property presented a means of putting the University's finances well into the black. Also, major outside funding was potentially available at the time.)

A site selection committee included Peter Stuart, an early 1950s MCC alumnus and a Foreign Service officer in the U.S. Embassy. The U.S. Government, as part of its foreign aid program, had decided to make a two-million-dollar grant to the University, and Peter Stuart "had the pleasure of working with [his] old professors as they explored various alternate sites. [He] jokingly told the Dean of the School of Business that there were not too many of the alumni who had been successful enough to make a two-million-dollar gift to the school."[8]

In "November, 1963, discussions began with Bruno Pagliai (husband of the late British and American actress Merle Oberon) concerning the donation of property in Lomas Verdes (reported as "by a group of Mexican and Italian industrialists") on which to build a new campus. In July, 1964, the committee announced that the new campus would be in Lomas Verde,"[9] dependent upon sufficient financing. Lomas Verde is located 7 miles NW of Mexico City, on the road to Ciudad Satelite. (Because of city growth, Ciudad Satelite is no longer a "satelite" to Mexico City.) A concentrated campaign to raise money for the UA Development Fund started. (See Note K for a list of the donations of record.)

Dr. Ray Lindley met with Don Manuel Espinosa Iglesias in September, 1965, to ask for a donation from the Mary Street Foundation. [Note D] Don Manuel countered by offering to give the *Colegio Americano de Puebla* to the University. (The *Colegio Americano de Puebla*, founded as a secondary school in Puebla in 1943 by Mrs. Anne Jenkins Buntzler, sister of William O. Jenkins, to teach English as a second language.) Five months later the Mary Street Foundation approved, and the University accepted, the donation of The Colegio to the University of the Americas. (In May, 1970, the University transferred *Colegio Americano* to the American School Foundation.[9] It is not known if any money was involved in the transfer.)

Again, Dr. Ray Lindley met with Don Manuel Espinosa Iglesias on July 19, 1966 to ask for a $8,000 donation from the Mary Street Foundation. It was at this meeting that Espinosa Iglesias inquired into having the University build and administer an Instituto Tecnológico de Puebla, in Puebla. Lomas Verde as a future campus site was immediately moved to the back burner. Lindley met with Fulton Freeman, American Ambassador in México, regarding the building of a new campus in Puebla rather than in Lomas Verde: "Would the Agency for International Development continue its support?"[9]

Following a series of positive meetings with, among others, Agustin Yañez, the Minister of Education, and Ing. García Roel, the Rector of the Instituto Tecnológico de Estudios Superiores de Monterrey, the Board of Trustees assembled to discuss the move to Puebla. Don Manuel Iglesias was in attendance to explain that the Mary Street Foundation would pay one-half the cost up to 5 million dollars. A week later, on October 26, 1966, the Board approved the move to Puebla by a margin of 17 to 1 (John Sevier). In January 25, 1967, two new members of the Board of Trustees took office: William D. Jenkins, Jr. and Dr. Sergio B. Guzmán. Two days later the University of the Americas publicly announced it will move to a new campus in Cholula, Puebla.[9]

The university purchased Sixty-Six hectares (163 acres) of land on the site of the old hacienda de Santa Catarina Martir (5 miles from the state capital, Puebla) from Maximino Avila Camacho, at seven pesos per square meter.[9] Currently (2005) the Puebla campus consists of 180 acres.

The first stone laid on the Cholula land was on June 4, 1967; and construction started early January, 1968.[9] The same year the school's name changed from the University of the Américas to the Universidad de las Américas. The actual move was scheduled for the fall of 1969, and the inauguration held in 1970.

MCC held the last graduation ceremony (for 106 graduates) on the Toluca highway campus in the theatre on May 29, 1970. James Farmer, Assistant Secretary for Administration of the U.S. Department of Health, Education and Welfare, was the commencement speaker. The school published the last issue of *The Collegian* there, and, as Professor Edward Simmen recently remarked, "We have never had a newspaper like that since." On June 4 the doors to the Mexico City campus closed officially.[9]

In March, 1970, a contract was signed to sell the km. 16 campus to the International University of the United States (formerly California Western University) for 7 million pesos.[9] The Carretera Mexico-Toluca campus site is now utilized by "CIDE," Centro de Investigación y Docencia Económicas, A.C. http://www.cide.edu/presentacion.html

Registration began on the new campus in Cholula on June 19, 1970. For the first time since 1942, beginning Mexican students during the following Fall semester outnumbered English-speaking freshman. This soon became important, because financing through the U.S. Government's AID program was only for ASHA projects (American Schools and Hospitals Abroad.) On July 1, 1971, Jess Dalton, Board President, Dr. Ray Lindley, and Manuel Espinoza Iglesias met in Washington with senators and congressmen regarding further financial assistance from the U.S. Government. Five months later AID donated $5,000,000.00.[9]

It is unknown for how long U.S. Government financial support for UDLAP continued after this date. [Note K]

In late 1985, "a handful of deans and faculty of the Universidad de las Américas in Puebla renounced their positions and created the Universidad de las Américas, A.C. (UDLA, A.C.) in Mexico City," at Avenida Puebla 223, Col. Roma. (Also see last paragraph in Note D.)

"While it was a matter of huge controversy, the Mexico City university took the same name and coat of arms of the Puebla institution (they have created a new coat of arms recently), and claimed to be successor of Mexico City College (in fact they added that title to their new coat of arms). Thus, both the Distrito Federal (DF) campus (UDLA, A.C.) and UDLA-Puebla campus laid claim to MCC as their founding institution."

After the split, the Puebla institution "officially registered itself as the Fundación Universidad de las Americas, Puebla" (UDLAP), mainly to distinguish itself from the new university in Mexico City. UDLAP is the university that still belongs to SACS and ... ranked among the top five universities in Mexico, not the UDLA, A.C." [14]

A UDLAP professor says, "[we] have absolutely no connection with that (D.F.) school, except for the fact that we share the first 45 years of existence."[9] And a former Board member of UDLA, A.C., adds, "It was a nasty split with much animosity."

So, despite a common origin, the Universidad de las Américas, A.C., Col. Roma, Mexico, DF, should not be confused with the Puebla institution. (http://www.udla.mx/2003/directorio.html) There is considerable difference in the size of the two Institutions, in the physical plant, the student and faculty, and endowment.

The DF institution enrollment for 1991-92 was 1,369, "mostly part time;" UDLAP enrollment for the same year "was 6,000 plus." It uses a similar logo as the UDLAP institution. Their web site states: "The Universidad de las Américas, A.C., founded in 1940 as Mexico City Junior College (MCC). In the next twenty-seven years its name changed, first as the University of the Américas, and later the Universidad de las Américas, A.C. (Asociación Civil)." Ten years later, in 2003, the student enrollment was 1,696; total faculty was 185 (36 full time).

On the other hand, in 2004, the UDLA-Puebla total students exceeded 8,000, with 1,647 new students admitted; and with 250 being international students (students from the U.S. comprising a "small minority"). Total faculty was 763; forty-four percent full time, while twenty percent belong to the National System of Researchers (SNI). UDLAP offers a Study Abroad Program at 182 universities in 29 countries, including an internship with the U.S. Congress. [Note E]

Many of the old Mexico City College crowd do not know to which university they belong as an alumnus. Numerous correspondence from 1996 to 2006 with the DF campus (from the president on down) by the author seeking alumni information received no response.

However, correspondence by the author over several years with the Puebla campus did result in several responses, e.g., "Thank you for calling this matter to our attention. We will look into it," but no substantial action was ever taken. Part of the reason could be that "until recent years, the Puebla campus never recognized . . . the association with Mexico City College. Now (02/22/05), they do" [11] . . . thanks to two fortuitous and coinciding events:

An MCC alumnus, Jed Linde, (MCC 1960, B.A.) wrote to the then Rectora, Dra. Nora Lustig, in September, 2002, asking about the status of MCC with the university. And, by happy coincidence, since taking office as Rectora in 2001, it was Dra. Nora Lustig's personal "...quest to do everything in our power to re-establish contact with our alumni from (the MCC) era." She wrote to Linde, "The letter you will receive from Sergio Diaz, who is in charge of our alumni office, is precisely the result of this initiative." [15]

Linde's inquiry gave Dra. Lustig a renewed interest as President to pursue her desire to promote UDLAP's early history and alumni. Soon after, Sergio Diaz, UDLAP exalumnos director, contacted Linde "...to discuss ways to facilitate MCC alumni participation in the UDLAP's exalumno program and to outline his ideas."

"Diaz is planning a special MCC section within the UDLAP exalumno site: http://www.udlap.mx/alumni/mcc/, (Ed. Note: It is now non-existent), and included a hyperlink within the UDLAP/MCC section to the (now defunct) MCC Yahoo club." [6]

Many have agreed that the education received at MCC prepared them well for their subsequent careers. As archaeology professor Oriol Pi-Sunyer

(MCC, 1954), at the University of Massachusetts-Amherst), recalls that his years in Mexico were "...the best thing that ever happened to me experientially, intellectually, and academically."

"Having the chance to live and study in Mexico City was adventure enough, but when all the natural and human landscapes of Mexico became part of the experiential classroom, the education that each of us received went far beyond anything most of us had anticipated. The college provided its students with a dynamic setting for intellectual and personal growth, and it offered unimaginable opportunities for exploration, discovery, adventure and creativity. The Mexican experience exposed its students, representing over 20 countries, to new ways to view their own countries. Life in Mexico helped all of us to develop a feeling for diversity and a belief that because of it, life can be richer and more meaningful." Wilkie, MCC,1959.[16]

MCC served us well, and gave birth to a highly prestigious institution. UDLAP recognizes MCC and its contributions and has named a building after Drs. Murray and Cain. Dr. Murray's son, Paul V. Murray, Jr., Ph.D., and his two sisters, were guests to its dedication (March 1, 1998). As Paul Murray's son wrote, "The Inauguration was truly a supreme and far-reaching gesture by UDLAP in recognition of its heritage and . . . honored his father's vision." [Note F]

Editor's Note:

UDLAP's website's MCC history consists of, "Universidad de las Américas Puebla was founded in 1940, in the nation's capital; it was known then as Mexico City College." Above it is a picture of the early DF MCC building, with some students and who may be Drs. Murray and Cain in the doorway:

There is, however: *Memorias 1940-1975, Universidad de las Americas.* An illustrated history in Spanish of MCC to UDLAP, with twenty pages devoted to MCC:

Also, UDLAP maintains a complete collection of the Collegian newspapers and its predecessors online at: and *The First 20 Years: 1940-1960,* an illustrated prospectus published by the college to raise funds.

During the creation of this book, I reached out to UDLAP and UDLA A.C. The response and the lack of one sum it up: They appear disinterested in having a connection with the history website, book, or the MCC Facebook group. So be it.

MCC was unique; offering more than an education through contact with multiple cultures and unique experiences. Many MCC students have commented favorably about how much their time at the school meant to them, and how fortunate they feel for attending MCC and living in Mexico.

-Jed Linde, 2024

References and Notes

1. "Yankee College in Mexico," L.R. Hayman. *Américas* 5:21-3 (May, 1953); The MCC Collegian, May 9, 1951.

2. "MCC, An Informal Report," Merle Kling. College and University. V. 33, No. 3:257-72. (Spring, 1958.)

3. "American Schools are Thriving in Mexico," Leonor A. Larew. *Hispania.* 63:91-93. (March, 1980.)

4. "Murray Would Be in Seventh Heaven," *El Universal.* Sept., 1998.

5. "Beards & Sandals Go," *Times Educational Supplement.* 2511:8, (July 5, 1963).

6. Jed Linde, in private email dated 3/6/2006.

7. "Yankee University in Mexico," Randolph Wolfe, *Holiday.* July, 1968.

8. Peter Tristan Stuart, former MCC alumnus and employee of the U.S. Embassy. See at http://westwood.fortunecity.com/susileib/60/pete18.htm [1](Chapter 19).

9. Professor Edward Simmen, Docente-Investigador, Deptos. de Lenguas y Literatura. UDLAP. Various correspondences.

10. "The Death of Joan V. Burroughs," James W. Grauerholz, American Studies Dept., Univ. of Kansas, January 7, 2002 (Note B) http://old.lawrence.com/burroughs/deathofjoan-full.pdf. (p. 42).

11. Earl R. Votaw (MCC,'52) February 22, 2005, correspondence.

12. Adapted from http://en.wikipedia.org/wiki/Mexico_City_College

13, (Post No. 1218 MCC Yahoo Grupo) Yahoo closed all groups, but this post may be available on the Wayback Machine.

14. J.Alonso. http://en.wikipedia.org/wiki/Talk:Fundaci%C3%B3n_Universidad_de_las_Am%C3%A9ricas%2C_Puebla.

15, (Post No. 328 MCC Yahoo Group). Yahoo closed all groups, but this message may be available on the Wayback Machine.

16. Richard Wilkie (MCC, 1959, Professor of Geography, University of Massachusetts-Amherst), "Dangerous Journeys: Mexico City College Students and the Mexican Landscape," *Adventures Into Mexico: American Tourism Beyond the Border.* Ed Nicholas Dagen Bloom (Rowman & Littlefield Pub,

---

1.   http://westwood.fortunecity.com/susileib/60/pete18.htm

Inc., 2006. profmex.org/mexicoandtheworld/volume11/4fall06/mcchap_final.htm

17. One of many notable alumni ('52) is Sra. Helen Escobedo. As related by Prof. Edward Simmen in a 1983 interview with Sra. Escobedo, at age 15 she approached Professor Wacher in 1950 and stated, "Buenas tardes. Soy Helen Escobedo y deseo estudiar arte." Wacher's response, "Let's see what we can do for you." Ms. Escobedo went on to establish an international reputation and served (1982-84) as the temporary Director for the Museum of Modern Art in Mexico City.

18. Herschel Brickell, "Writers' Workshop," <u>Americas</u>, Jan. 1952. p.19.

19. Crawford Kilian, unpublished memoir, *"Growing up Blacklisted,"* 1990, as quoted by Diana Anhalt, *"Bridging the Culture Gap, from A Gathering of Fugitives," <u>Adventures Into Mexico: American Tourism Beyond the Border</u>*. ed. Nicholas D. Bloom (Rowman & Littlefield Pub, Inc., 2006) p. 156. See 16, above. The life of Cold-war repatriates, the Hollywood Blacklist, and international refugees in Mexico City is also well covered by Diana Anhalt's first-hand account, <u>A Gathering of Fugitives: American Political Expatriates in Mexico 1948-1965</u>. (Archer Books, 2001.) This account was excerpted in "Bridging The Culture Gap," *ibid*.

20. "The MCC Collegian," June 8, 1961.

21. <u>The First 20 Years: 1940-1960</u>, published by Mexico City College, 1960, as a 26-page prospectus to raise funds for future expansion.

A. Prof. Edward Simmen (UDLAP).

B. "The Death of Joan V. Burroughs," by James W. Grauerholz. American Studies Dept., Univ. of Kansas, January 7, 2002:

"A strange thing—as Ed Simmen pointed out to me—is that, in all the contemporaneous Mexico City newspaper accounts (22 stories examined to date), there is not one single mention of Mexico City College. And yet, the killer, one of the eyewitnesses, the young man who came by to consider buying a pistol from Burroughs, the boy who identified Joan's body, and the tenant in whose apartment the shooting occurred—all were currently or recently students enrolled at MCC. The Bounty bar, almost entirely patronized by a certain subset of MCC students; while the entire 122 Monterrey building was full of them." -Joseph M. Quinn, 2006

Just as clubby was the world of the college's American founders, President Henry L. Cain and Dean of Faculty, Paul V. Murray. Although MCC's finances were a tremendous struggle in the early years, and Dean Murray even mortgaged his home to support the school at one point, these two men were well connected within a middle to lower rung of the American-Mexican 'old-boy network.' And this, at a time when Mexico was relatively supine beneath the postwar American business invasion. Murray and Cain had power, and—thanks to their primary patrons, the Jenkins Foundation—money. If they did not want their school mentioned in newspaper accounts of a lurid, scandalous killing, it was surely within their ability to see that it did not happen. Of course, the American G.I. 'colony' in Colonia Roma did not usually command wide journalistic attention in DF — except when it brought out a story like this one. Perhaps the reporters were simply uninterested in the MCC connection; or perhaps their editors operated at that time under a general policy of not offending the American institutions established in Mexico. If Dr. Simmen's theory is correct, Murray or Cain must have somehow exerted influence on editors who were specifically looking to scandalize or discredit MCC—and that is possible." http://old.lawrence.com/burroughs/deathofjoan-full.pdf. (p. 42.)

C. Robert Barlow fell ill shortly thereafter and forced to take a leave of absence. The following year, 1951, he died.

(Professor Wigberto Jiménez Moreno offered the first anthropology course on September 30, 1947. The first student to register in anthropology was Walter Madson, a WW II veteran, under the G.I. Bill.[9])

"*The 2nd edition,* published in 1950, and edited by Barlow's assistant, Leon Abrams, Jr (graduate student). Articles included works by Barrios, Horcasitas, Pedro Armillas, Eduardo Noguera, Ignacio Bernal, Patricia Fent Ross, Donald Kimmel, and Wigberto Jiménez Moreno. (Jiménez Moreno and Pedro Bosch Gimpera had founded the Dept. of Anthropology at MCC in 1947.)

John Paddock, who first came to MCC as a graduate student in 1951, became the editor in 1952. *Issue No. 3,* published in October, 1953, had an expansion on a single theme, *Excavaciones in the Mixteca Alta,* which consisted of reports on student field work. Written by Paddock, the issue contained materials provided by Robert Winter and Francis Guess and participating students: Tikey Magionos, Frank Moore, Robert Wiley, Lee Arnett, Arthur Parker, and Herbert Nell. A graduate student from USC and Paddock provided photographs and Charles Wicke was responsible for the drawings.

Issue No. 4 did not appear until December 1955. Tom Swinson was the editor and his assistant was Donald Brockington. Paddock was not the faculty advisor since he had joined the staff in 1953. This issue, dedicated to the excavations made at *Yagul, Oaxaca*, was the first in a series of reports of MCC's work at this site. It contains work by Fernando Horcasitas, Richard George, John Paddock, James Oliver, C. Chard Meigs, and others.

The 5th edition came out two years later in August 1957. also edited by Swinson and Brockington, and continued the emphasis on the work in Oaxaca and at *Yagul*. Articles were by Paddock, Charles Wicke, Horcasitas, Brockington, and Irmgard W. Johnson.

The next issue did not appear until 1965 due to the considerable turmoil at all levels of the College including changes of the president and even changes of the name of the College to the University of the Américas. *Issue 6* was also very different from the previous issues in that it dealt with reviews of books published by Oscar Lewis and reviewed by John Paddock: *Five Families, The Children of Sanchez, Pedro Martínez: A Mexican Peasant and His Family*. The issue was going to be a text for classes at the University. This was also the time when the Attorney General of Mexico accused Oscar Lewis of writing obscene literature and sent the Mexican press into an uproar.

"A double issue, *No. 7 & 8*, appeared the following year and returned to the original format used by Barlow. This issue, dedicated to the XI Round Table of the *Sociedad Mexicana de Antropología*, held in México City in August of 1966. The great site of Teotihuacan was the special topic. John Paddock was again editing <u>Mesoamerican Notes</u>, and he selected graduate thesis on Teotihuacan written over the years at MCC and UDLA. Authors included Robert Chadwick, Will T. Levey, Frank Moore, and Evelyn C. Rattray. Paddock's assistants for this issue were Estelle Keller, Joseph Moger, Andrea Wakefield and Iris Hart.

The same year, 1966, John Paddock left UDLA and became director of the *Instituto de Estudios Oaxaqueños* in Mitla, Oaxaca. Paddock also published *Ancient Oaxaca*.

It was not until Fall of 1983 that the *9th edition* of the journal appeared with the name, *Notas Mesoamericanas*. The editor was now Edward Simmen and the issue dedicated to Dr. Wigberto Jiménez Moreno and Dr. John Paddock."

(The brief description above by Dr. Mike Porath is based on material from the Preface of the 9th edition of Mesoamerican Notes, written by Dr. Edward Simmen, and included in its entirety because of the importance archaeology has played with MCC, and for the students and teachers involved, Joseph M. Quinn.)

D. The late U.S. citizen William O. Jenkins, of Puebla, MX, was "a mysterious buccaneer businessman who has built the biggest personal fortune in Mexico," (Time, Dec 26, 1960. p.25), and established (1954) the Mary Street Jenkins Foundation, in honor of his wife, for the benefit of the Mexican people, specifically for Puebla. Jenkins "left very little of his money to his family, endowing instead the Foundation. By 1988, the Foundation had provided more than $150 million for education, culture, health, welfare (including orphan schools) and sports through more than 300 specific grants." Of his many profitable ventures, Jenkins purchases of local banks culminated in the establishment of one of the largest banks in Latin America, Bancomer.

"In 1963 I calculated that the Mary Street Jenkins Foundation then bore the same ratio to the Mexican economy as did the Rockefeller Foundation to the US economy." (Luke Case on Bill Jenkins: see http://www.dartmouth/, next link below.)

Enter the ghost of Juan Hernandez: UDLAP was first run by a banker, Manuel Espinosa Yglesias, who also headed the Jenkins Foundation. In subsequent years, Yglesias managed to expel members of the Jenkins family from the Board of the Foundation, taking control of it and the Campus.[11] Bill Jenkins countered with legal action in Federal court and "After a seven-year struggle, he regained control of the Mary Street Jenkins Foundation." (www.dartmouth.org/classes/54/Newsletter/NL0307.htm[2]. July, 2003).

This resulted in restoring the Foundation to its original status and the school to its rightful academic administration.

---

2.   http://www.dartmouth.org/classes/54/Newsletter/NL0307.htm

(For a summary of how President Macias Rendon, (1975-76), changed UDLAP from a liberal arts institution into a technocratic institution to provide job training for engineers, and the decade-long battle to reverse the trend, see 16—Wilkie, ibid, p. 95.)

Nor has the small DF campus been exempt from avarice. The 91-year-old American author Russell Abbot Ames was fighting for his right to stay on disputed land in *San Pablo Etla*, a tiny village in the mountains above Oaxaca. He says that although he and his wife donated their 20-acre homestead to the university in 1988, they did so with the agreement that they could live there until they died. Because of a technicality (his wife died first), the DF campus attempted to immediately evict the 91-year-old American, resulting in his temporary incarceration; a man who has shared so much of his good fortune with the Mexican people.

E. UDLA-Puebla is the only institution outside the United States that has a program whereas its students serve as U.S. Congressional interns in Washington, DC, "While (then Congressman Bill Richardson and I visited in Washington, DC), I noticed the students serving as interns. I asked him if he would take a couple from the UDLAP. He said, 'I think it is against the law.' Yes, we found out it is. You can't have foreigners 'working' in Congress because there is so much confidential material they must work with. And, of course, our students can't work because they have no papers. (We say our students 'serve' in the office of Congressmen.) Also, it is against the Mexican constitution for a Mexican to 'work' for a foreign government. Oh, well, we do it anyway. The students get the added benefit of meeting with the Mexican ambassador to the US while they are there. It is a marvelous and successful program. I really enjoy having initiated it. Such students!" (—Dr. Edward Simmen.[9])

F. Dr. Paul V. Murray's son (Paul V. Murray, Jr., Ph.D. Education) writes, ". . . my father's idealism got in the way of making clear and difficult decisions which eventually ended his administration."

(But it is such idealism, which gives birth to dreams that can blossom beyond expectations. Ironically, all too often, once matured, effective maintenance and growth then requires the skills of a "non-dreamer;" such skills are usually at odds to nurturing a dream from its infancy, Joseph M. Quinn.)

G. William B. Richardson, Jr., a Governor of New Mexico [former Congressman, and former Ambassador to the UN] and the son of William B. Richardson (former MCC Board of Trustees Chair) attended MCC as a high school student for one summer, and then attended "another school" in Mexico City. Mr. Richardson was the Commencement Speaker at the Universidad de las Américas-Puebla 2003 Graduation Ceremonies, and awarded a Honoris Causa Degree. (See Note H, below.)

H. William Richardson, Sr., MCC Board of Trustees Chair, and forcibly removed from the board, as noted in this letter dated July 14, 1961, and sent from Frank A. Tredennick Jr to Dr. Nils Y. Wessell (who at the time was president of Tufts University. http://www.wargs.com/political/richardson.html):

"I had a long discussion this week with Fred J. Lauerman, executive assistant to the president of Mexico City College. He reported to me that Mexico City College had made its greatest stride forward in years by forcibly deposing Bill Richardson from the board of trustees. The general feeling, however, is that the action came too late and that Richardson's leadership has been so misdirected and yet so strong that the College will probably go under in the next year or two."

I. *The Gadfly*, an alternative student newspaper, published by Peter and Lucia Montague, had only four issues, the last in December 1961. "There were two bombshell stories in this last issue. First was the fact that the Michigan State University system had announced that they were no longer accepting credits from MCC, thereby ending Michigan's involvement in the 'Winter Quarter in Mexico' program." (NOTE: The author has not been able to corroborate this story.)

The other articles involved the so-called "Foot Sniffing Certificate," which ridiculed the Dean of Men, as well as the policies and personalities of the Mexican Government. This latter volley sent the Federales looking for anyone mentioned in *The Gadfly* article, most were residents of *Cuajimalpa* and *Contadero*. No arrests occurred, mainly because, by happy chance, several had already left for their ritual fun and games in Acapulco.

Like most "bomb throwers," the publishers of *The Gadfly* left the country before the last issue appeared.

J. ¨MCC stands about 900 feet above the Valley of Mexico on a prominence known as *La Angostura* (the Narrow Point). This neck of land separates the ravine of *Tlapecho* on the north from that of *Cuitlapechco* on the south, the latter flanked on one side by precipitous sand cliffs called *Peñablanca*. These lands lie in an area known in *Aztec* times as the Province of *Cuahuacan*, and are now incorporated into the township of Santa Fe, D.F.¨ Possibly more so than any other area surrounding the Valley, this prominence "reflects the multicultural and multilingual history of the nation: this vantage point has witnessed the early semi-nomadic *Otomí* life along with their peaceful neighbors the *Matlatzinca*, the great expansion of the Aztec Empire and their annual, great hunt on this prominence where the college now stands, the 16th-Century Conquest and the colonization and missionary efforts (including the extraordinary Utopian project of Santa Fe, located just below the college, undertaken by Don Vasco de Quiroga, the remarkable first bishop of Michoacán), and the wars of Independence, the witnessing of departure and arrival of many a military expedition along a three-hundred year old Indian road that passed through the area, the years of political upheaval and, finally, a successful experimental international educational institute,¨ the Mexico City College. Adapted from Fernando Horcasitas, *"Cuauhtlalpan,"* <u>The Collegian</u>, Dec. 17, 1955.

K. Donations to UDLA covering twenty years between August 1963 to October 1983 totaled a minimum of $21,450,800. Most of these donations went to support the move, construction, and continuing support of the Puebla campus. (Source, footnote 9, above.)

1. Lilly Endowments, Inc., Indianapolis, Indiana: $45,000, for a Chair of Economics at the UDLA campus, plus $75,000 as a general grant.

2. Relm Foundation, Ann Arbor, Michigan: $4,800 to underwrite the salary for an economics professor; and $105,000 for faculty salaries.

3. The Lora Lavery Stafford Scholarship Fund was established with the donation of $46,000 from her estate. (The fund, however, disappeared over the years.)

4. The Scaiffe Family Foundation, Philadelphia: $250,000 for the campus.

5. The Gildred Family Foundation, San Diego, CA: $250,000.

6. The Frank B. Baird, Jr. Foundation, $75,000, for professors to continue research.

7. U.S. Government Agency for International Development (AID):

a. $2,000,000 to help build a new campus.

b. $2,000,000 (dependent upon a match of $1,400,000).

c. $1,600,000 (funneled through the University of Americas Foundation, Delaware, RI(?) donated as $285,923,273.74 pesos).

d. $5,000,00 (Dec. 17, 1971). The Foundación Jenkins (the Mary Street Jenkins Foundation?) agreed to match the grant.

8. The Mary Street Foundation, Puebla, MX (see Note D, above. $5,000,000, plus the Colegio Americano de Puebla.

9. Richard Ware, president of the Ann Arbor, MI based Earhart Foundation, was the speaker for the first graduation ceremony (54 graduates) held on the Cholula campus. (Amount of donation, if any, unknown.)

10. Dr. Ray Lindley named Chancellor, with offices in San Antonio, TX in charge of planning, development and relations with U.S. foundations.

L. American Football at MCC/UDLA, by Professor Edward Simmen (UDLAP), see Citation 9, above.

"Prior to 1947, there was very little interest in having organized sports. The school had no facilities for organized sports and the enrollment was sparse. As more veterans began to arrive to study at MCC, interest in having an American football team intensified which pleased Paul Murray who felt that having a team would bring recognition to the community. Throughout the spring and summer quarters, the veterans began playing informally together. They were all former college football players.

During the summer of 1947, MCC (Aztecas) applied for entry and was accepted to play in the country's Liga Mayor to play in the fall against the six other local teams in the league: the UNAM, the Instituto Politécnico, Colegio Militar, Educación, Y.M.C.A, and Wacha-chara. Coach Chuck LaTourette, who also played, began the season with defeats by the UNAM and Politecnico.

In the first game, following only one week of practice due to late arrival of players and equipment, the UNAM won 20-0. The Instituto Politecnico defeated MCC with the score of 7-0. These losses resulted from scheduling the two strongest teams for the start of the season.

Colegio Militar was defeated 13-0. Educacion went down 13-7 in a night contest—which marked the Aztecs first appearance in the Olympic stadium—and YMCA was routed 32-7 in the last conference game of the year. MCC placed third in the conference standings.

With only a few exceptions, the majority of the MCC players were veterans of World War II, studying at MCC on the GI Bill, and were much older than the average beginning students. All of them had experience playing football at universities in the United States such as UCLA, Illinois, and the University of California before entering the service. Among the players were Joe Roldan, Jack Smith, Pop Muldoon, Bud Fellows, Dick Ehrhardt, Nick Lococo, Seymour Barkowitz, Vic Hancock and Eddie Armador.

One of the most outstanding players was Morris "Moe" Williams, from Alabama. 'Moe' was the only Negro on the team, a factor that would cause an unexpected problem near the end of the 1947 season, and MCC ventured out of Mexico City to play two postseason games.

For the first postseason game, the team, accompanied by Paul Murray, ventured to Monterrey to play the ITESM. The Aztecas overwhelmed the Tecnologico 33-7.

Then, the team travelled to San Antonio, Texas to play Trinity University. When they arrived in the Alamo City, Dean Murray shockingly discovered that Texas had laws that prevented Negroes playing on the same field as whites. However, he was determined that his one Negro player, 'Moe' Williams was not going to miss playing simply because he was Black.

After some thought, Murray came up with a plan: First, he had the team suit up at the hotel. Then, they went by chartered bus to the stadium. All the players wore their helmets to help disguise 'Moe,' and raced into the dressing room and then on to the field. 'Moe' wore his helmet the entire game, removing it only in the dressing room during halftime. As part of Murray's plan to hide the fact that 'Moe' was a Negro, Murray had the Alabama native listed in the program as being a Mexican from Mexico City. But that simply added to a greater problem. Considering that San Antonio had a large Mexican and

Mexican-American population, there would be many of them who would go to the game to see Mexico City College play. Both Murray and 'Moe' worried, "What if someone speaks to 'Moe' in Spanish?" 'Moe' had been in Mexico a short period of time. What Spanish he had was rudimentary to say the least. So, it was decided that the entire team would protect 'Moe.' He spent the entire game not only wearing his helmet, but also remaining absolutely silent.

Aside from all of that, the game was a total disaster for the Aztecas of MCC. Trinity University ran rampant over MCC by a score of 73 to 6.

Nevertheless, one person found solace amid such a devastating defeat. A writer for the 1948 yearbook noted, 'The Trinity game was the first time a Negro—Williams—played among whites on a Texas gridiron.' The Aztecs may have been crushed on the field, but 'they made history.'

The season did not end there for two of the Aztecas Warriors: 'Moe' Williams and Bud Fellows. They were both selected to play with the Mexican All-Stars against the Randolph Field Air Force Base team in the 'Silver Bowl' in Mexico City before a crowd of 35,000 spectators, the largest crowd in local football history. With the great help of Williams and fellows, the Mexican All-Stars surprised the Randolph Field team by defeating them 24-21.

With John D. Engman as Coach, the Aztecas won the national America-Football championship by defeating the Pumas of the UNAM 32-26, reportedly in one of the most exciting games in the history of American football in Mexico. Among the outstanding players for the Aztecs was Morris 'Moe' Williams.

"Between 1947 and 1954, American-Football was MCC's only intercollegiate sport. Strong rivalries rose between the UNAM and the Politecnico teams. Then, President Murray withdrew the team from the 'Liga Mayor' prior to the beginning of the 1955 season. He noted, 'Local conditions would have to change greatly before the college would consider re-entry into the league.'

'Moe' Williams graduated from MCC in 1950, but he did not leave Mexico. Rather, he opened a travel agency catering to American tourists. However, he remained close to MCC and President Murray.

Members of the Mexico City College *Aztecas* varsity softball team, Fall 1957

Left to right:
Standing: **John Freeman** (Boise, Idaho), Joe Palistrami (New York City), **Bob "Booner" Hunter** (Boise, Idaho & Honolulu, Hawaii), "Country" Ken Posner (Alice Springs, Texas), Pierce Travis (Brooklyn, NY), John Niemi (Milwaukee, Wisc.), Peter Schnabel (Chicago), Stew Fall (Detroit), Joe Chase (Marsing, Idaho) and Bill Hornaday (Washington, D.C.)
Front row: Tony Perez (El Paso, Texas), Del Theasmeyer (Lincoln, Neb.), Ted Turner (Nashville, Tenn.), **Dick Wilkie** (Boise, Idaho), and Manager Fred Williams (Pomona, California).

In 1955, MCC fielded a softball team, playing in the Inter-Club Softball league and finishing in second place. In 1956, the team entered the new "Liga Mayor" Softball League and promptly won the championship. MCC softball varsity teams continued playing in the "Liga Mayor" from that time well into the late 1960s.

A number of MCC students played in the 'Liga Mayor' for the Military College (Academia Militarizada Mexico) team during the 1957-58 and 1958-59 seasons. (See an account of some games and several team photos in footnote 16), and the MCC Collegian newspaper covered a number of the games, especially by reporter Pierce Travis.) MCC players included Pete Schnabl, Dick Wilkie, Ben Madrid, Tony Perez, Ronnie Daniels and Eddie Mack.

At the same time, MCC played basketball as an intramural sport. By 1958, MCC's basketball team entered that sport's 'Liga Mayor'. The individual who volunteered to coach the team without remuneration was none other than

'Moe' Williams. He remained coach until forced by illness to resign in 1990. He died the following year.

In 1962, Dr. D. Ray Lindley became the third president of MCC, promising to restore American football at the intercollegiate level. This did not happen. However, he did continue to support the basketball team, keeping Williams as coach.

UDLA has won numerous national championships after its move to Puebla. Basketball players, recruited from the United States, were all very tall and towered over the average Mexican players on other teams. That led to the national authorities passing a law that there could be only one foreign basketball player on the court at one time." — Professor Edward Simmen (UDLAP)

Resources and Reading

The Collegian:

Fourteen Volumes of The *MCC Collegian*, representing 199 issues, 3-11-49 to 5-14-63, were among the sources accessed in the compilation of this History. The digitalized issues are online in PDFs.

There are also links to the Collegian's predecessors: *El Conquistador de Mexico City College* 7-9-47 to 2-28-48, and *El Grito de Mexico City College, and The First 20 Years: 1940-1960*, an illustrated prospectus published by the college to raise funds, at: http://catarina.udlap.mx/u_dl_a/acervos/mcc/mcc_1940_1960.pdf

MCC Yahoo Group:

Unfortunately, the Yahoo MCC alumni *grupo* site, founded by Mike Porath [MCC 1959, BA] on September 1, 2000, no longer exists. Yahoo closed all its groups in December 2020 with nothing archived. Apparently, there is a collection of the Yahoo MCC group posts at Internet Archive, The Wayback Machine, but I found the site frustratingly difficult to locate them

MCC Facebook Group:

360-plus members at: https://www.facebook.com/groups/mexicocitycollege

Mexico City College History Website: https://mexicocitycollege.com/

Memorias 1940-1975, Universidad de las Americas. An illustrated history in Spanish of MCC to UDLAP. *https://issuu.com/webudlap/docs/memorias-udlap-80-anios*

*Dangerous Journeys: Mexico City College Students and the Mexican Landscape, 1954-1962,*Chapter 9 in Bloom, Nicolas (Ed.), *Adventures into Mexico : American Tourism beyond the Border* , Rowman & Littlefield , New York, 88-115. Republished at <u>Mexico and the World</u>, Volume 11, No.4 (Fall

2006) by PROFMEX and the UCLA Program on Mexico. Wilkie, R. 2006. At: profmex.org/mexicoandtheworld/volume11/4fall06/mccchap_final.htm

Our Formative Years and Mexico City College: 1952-1961, Vol. 25, Text and Photos Slides, Wilkie, R. and Oriol Pi-Sunyer, (2020) at: https://www.profmex.org/mexicoandtheworld/volume25/ 11earliestsummer2020/ Our_Formative_Years_and_Mexico_City_College_1952-1961.pdf

"Urban Growth and the Transformation of the Settlement Landscape of Mexico: 1910-1970," in *Contemporary Mexico: Papers of the IV International Congress of Mexican History*, Wilkie, R. 1976. (Univ. of California Press and El Colegio de Mexico, both English and Spanish editions, 99-134.

Latin American Population and Urbanization Analysis: Maps and Statistics, 1950-1982, Wilkie, Richard W. (1985 and 1990). UCLA Latin American Center Publications, (hardcover 1985) and (paperback 1990), 433 pages. The chapters on Mexico—pages 3-31 and 320-351—include 19 maps and cartograms of population historically.

Gringos in Mexico, a short story anthology, edited by Edward Simmen (1988).

Mexico City College Map

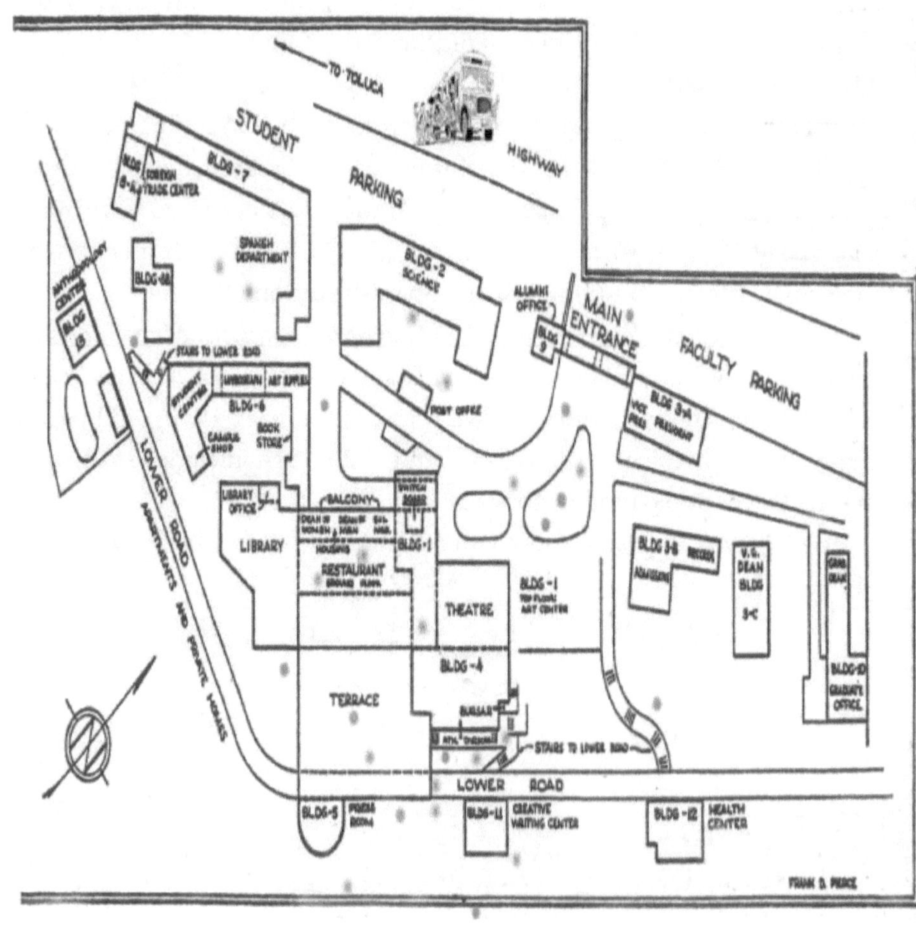

Mexico City College Photos

The Carretera Mexico-Toluca, Km.16 Campus, 1954-1973

The original College Building (1940-1954).

The Campus — College Theater and Main Entrance

CAMPUS SCENE—
ADMISSIONS
OFFICE

asses   Mexico City College Restaurant

Mosaic Mural by College Post Offic

Foreign Trade Center Quadrangle
FOREIGN TRADE

South Campus — Relaxing After Classes

Spanish Department Building

Spanish classes
are taught by bilingual instructors.

Reference Room — M.C.C. Library

Art Center Painting Studio

CAMPUS FIESTA

Student Poetry Club

MCC BUILDINGS overlook the highway which rises from the town of Santa Fe (Acaxochic) to Cuajimalpa and which was once the roadway to Tzintzunzan, Patzcuaro. For three hundred years it was used by the scores of Indian nations scattered along the west coast of Mexico as far north as Alaska.

Front quad is planted with colorful shrubs and paved in rose-
colored flagstones.

Chatting on Sun Terrace

Monika Howell, 1957

STUDENTS
LEAVING
ENGINEERING
BUILDING

Women students live in carefully supervised Mexican homes.

"Nos vemos en los Estados Unidos," banter (left to right) Samuel C. Ormes, Jr., Richard E. Henderson, Stanley R. Clayton, and Thomas C. Canfield outside the Spanish Department where they spent many hours learning the intricacies of the Spanish language.

Buildings of MCC's campus are connected by tree-shaded walks.

With Paul Estason in the lead, James Pechewlys, Max Connor, John Nowak, Lawrence Nowak, and Davy Minge go down the stairs for a last look around the anthropology lab.

YOUNG BUSJUMPER—Pete Carmichael takes the rare opportunity of a completely-stopped Toluca "rocket" to illustrate

"All right. You can have your Faulkner and I'll stick with Hemingway—all the way!" argues Robert W. Sparks, (right) as he and Robert E. Dunbar leave the writing center and one of their last discussions on American Literature.

Mural designed and painted by Norman Bradley, 1959

Joseph M. Quinn photos, 1956-1960.

"If you really feel that strongly about the article, send in a reply. This is your last chance, you know," says Arnus A. Valavicius (standing) to Robert C. Story (far left) and State Congressman Carl Minette.

The lawn below the terrace is a quiet spot to talk about old times for William Gowen and Don Arneson (standing); Kathleen Kelly and David Soblin (seated).

Mexico City College
And
Universidad de las Americas
Alumni
Memoirs

Martha (Hoyt) Turbie

I arrived at MCC as a transfer student in September of 1961, after receiving my A.A. from a "junior college" in Virginia the previous June. Having lived in a dorm that housed mostly foreign exchange students, in addition to having accompanied my Cuban roommate to Havana during spring break of 1960, the travel bug bit me hard. Instead of transferring to U VA as planned, I found an MCC catalog in the school library and decided to apply. My parents went along with it, as the tuition/living costs were lower (even factoring in the flights to and from NYC). They consulted with a friend whose wife was Mexican, and decided that it probably would be "safe" enough. The rest is history.

Majoring in Cultural Anthropology at MCC, I was a member of the first graduating class of the University of The Americas in June, 1963; at which, Rufino Tamayo received an honorary degree. Without fully realizing it at the time, I now know I studied under some of the most important Mesoamericanists of the last 75 years. John Paddock, Fernando Horcasitas, Remy Bastien, and more at MCC, also, Jose Garcia-Payon, the archaeologist in charge of the Tajin excavations in Vera Cruz. Later, I met Michael Coe, the Mayanist and curator emeritus of the Anthro collection at Yale. He authenticated some Pre-Columbian pottery shards I had snuck back with me from Central Mexico, and we corresponded in the last few years of his life. I cannot put a price on these and many other experiences that gave me so much "material" for great stories. In fact, a few of us may even share some of the same memories!

Except for a summer in Jalapa at the U of Veracruz, picking up the missing credits I needed to graduate, I lived in MCC student housing. First, on Michelet and Descartes in Anzures; then, Melchor O'Campo in Cuauhtemoc; and finally on Blvd. Xola in Narvarte. This last arrangement, with a family originally from Manila, was not by the college but through mutual friends. They became like family to me, and I am still in contact with their children and grandchildren on Facebook. I threw a wonderful graduation party at that house, inviting everyone I knew from ALL walks of life and persuasions. People still talk about it!

Not wanting to leave Mexico that Fall, I enrolled in Spanish Lit. grad classes. On November 22, 1963, the day President Kennedy was shot in Texas, I was enroute from the wedding of good friends to their reception at a Reforma restaurant. No one wanted to tell the bride and groom what had happened, but the news leaked out anyway and put a little damper on things. That December, I visited the happy couple in Costa Rica, and was just in time for an eruption of the Irazu volcano!

Money running out and discouraged by a D in an Economics elective, I returned to the states. Between 1965 and 1968, I held Spanish Language and ESL teaching jobs in Texas, NY, and Mass., while continuing grad work when I could. I collected enough eclectic credits for a M.A. but never received it, and left Mexico just before the Olympics in 1968. I married in 1969, worked for a personnel agency, accompanied my husband to grad school in New Mexico, worked for a Jewelry manufacturer, and probably found my true calling in 1979, when I started to work my way up in the newspaper business, wearing many hats for the next 30-some years. In 2019, Hearst Media bought out the family-based newspaper group where I worked, and many old-timers, myself included, were given the polite boot.

I would say my time in Mexico during the 60's shaped my life in incalculable ways. My worldview certainly reflects it. I am proud to be a member of such an "elite" group of dinosaurs.

Stephen Vollmer

When I first visited the campus in 1964, I met with a cadre of friends, who were attending classes up on the "hill." My immediate impression was of the international atmosphere of the wide-array of professors and students, who came from diverse backgrounds from within Mexico, Europe, Near East, Asia; Canada, and the United States.

After enrolling in 1966, initial classes led to a B.A., and then an M.A., focused on the Arts and Cultural History of the Americas and Europe (B.A. and M.A., 1966-72), and later to employment at UDLA (*Asesor Cultural* and Instructor, 1999-2004).

The MCC/UA experience set the stage, which became a lifetime of exploring locales and listening to many subjects, whose folk knowledge and lore are conveniently simplified or ignored by many scholars who have little if any true field experience. We were a lucky lot to have had others to show us the ropes.

For me, MCC/UA provided the ideal foundation for what became my lifelong career in museum administration, which concentrated on the organization of numerous exhibitions and programs, including the negotiation of loans of art and artifacts, documents, and other resources.

All said and done, most of these endeavors introduced and exposed museum visitors to new ideas and the ever-changing perspectives of past and present cultural facets found throughout the Americas.

While living in Mexico City, it was pleasure to have resided in several locales along with other students, which provided the opportunity to explore it via the trams, *peseros*, and on foot. Many European friends (who were working in Mexico at the time) and I enjoyed day trips and/or week-end jaunts to explore archaeological and historical sites throughout much of Central Mexico, well beyond the DF.

One such all-day adventure took us to Malinalco and Chalma (Estado de Mexico), then accessed on a road of crushed boulders that exemplified the plight of Penitentes (those doing penance), who walked from distant places as described in an old *bolero*. My German companions were determined to visit the sites, and penance was dispensed to the undercarriage of their car, when it suffered considerable damage.

Mexico City was a great and sophisticated playground, filled with wonderful museums and performance centers where, at affordable prices, we could enjoy many aspects of world culture. Then, there was the great variety of one-peso taco joints, and formal restaurants, cafes, nightclubs, and bars that seemed to be around every corner. Often, we gathered outside of the classrooms with numerous friends and professors, who introduced us to well-known scholars, diplomats, artists, along with well-respected members of the business and financial community.

It was a golden era, a very special time and place, one not likely to be repeated in the world of today's current affairs.

Postscript:

September 1, 2024: Listening to the radio this morning, a station played "Granada" by Agustin Lara who, during the mid-60's, we found playing and singing in the bar of a small Mexico City hotel called the Guadalupe.

Needless to say, we returned many a time to watch and listen to an amazing talent, who sat at the piano knocking out his tunes. All the gals, our dates included, swooned over his lyrical poetry, and we all marveled in near awe as he sat with a cigarette in the corner of his mouth singing away.

A mixed drink was ever present, resting on the piano. Between sets, cocktail in hand, he would chat with the audience, and ask if they had special requests. At the time, he was much older than us, yet timeless! Such good memories!!!

Note: Recognized as one of the most popular songwriters of his era, Ángel Agustín María Carlos Fausto Mariano Alfonso del Sagrado Corazón de Jesús Lara y Aguirre del Pino, known as Agustín Lara, (1897 to 1970) was a Mexican composer and performer of songs and boleros. Wikipedia[1]

---

1.   *https://en.wikipedia.org/wiki/Agust%C3%ADn_Lara*

Brian Mayne

UA attendance 1968 – 71 – Diploma in Industrial Administration, B.A. in Business Administration – *cum laude* (Dec. '69), B.A. in English Literature – *summa cum laude* (Spring '70), and MBA (Summer '71).

For some of 1969-70 I was part-time assistant to William Rodgers, Registrar and Director of Adult Education, and in 1969 acted as lab assistant in Prof. Teyssier's evening business statistics class.

Memories:

UA and Mexico are interwoven in memory and feelings. My time there was during very formative years, and deep and lasting impressions are still with me. UA's student body was a colourful salsa of new and old-world cultures with a kaleidoscope of psychological states shared by the characters then present. I was broadened as much, if not more, by exposure to this wide spectrum of eclectic students and the personalities and backgrounds of my professors than from the formal studies themselves.

Professors who especially stand out in memory for me are Coley Banks Taylor and Marjorie Henshaw (Creative Writing and English), Melvin Pine and Fred Schloesser (Business Administration), Mother Michel (Philosophy), Laurens Perry (History), General Carlos Berzunza (Geography).

Being with fellow students outside of the Km 16 campus in the Mexico of that time was always an adventure – on romantic dates in the Zona Rosa and Chapultepec Park, at restaurants sampling exotic flavours and textures, experiencing the colours and smells of the fruits, vegetables and the *brujas'* herbal remedies and spells at the markets, exploring some of the country's ancient foundations at the *Museo de Antropologia* and the pyramids, savouring the life and sounds of the floating gardens of Xochimilco, hearing the passionate Mariachi music in Garibaldi Plaza, the spa baths of Ixtapan de la Sal, and – later - visits to the impressive new campus in Cholula. I loved the atmosphere at the San Angel Inn, and a favourite restaurant was La Lorraine in an old colonial house near the earlier downtown MCC building, run by an older French woman of character with gray hair in a bun who prepared the authentic French cuisine.

Employment:

Management accounting at Massey Ferguson, accounting for their Canadian property and comptroller at their foundry, Ontario (71-74);

Canada Mexico Exchange Program trainee, Nacional Financiera, Mexico City (74-76);

Management consulting with Laventhol and Horwath mostly to the garment industry in several Canadian provinces, Toronto (76-80) and at

Booz Allen and Hamilton (now Strategy & under PwC) for automotive manufacturing clients internationally, London, UK (83-87);

Publishing, freelance consulting and volunteer management, London (87-01),

legal representative acting for asylum seekers and refugees at the charity Refugee Legal Centre, Dover, UK (02-07).

Looking back on the above, it turns out that since graduating from UA, I've lived in 23 homes in 5 countries on 3 continents, worked for approximately 100 companies in 16 countries and, in the last job, represented about 500 refugees and asylum seekers from 66 countries – with more than half of whom we were successful in their applications to stay in the UK and have their families join them.

Outside of my formal employment much of the passing decades were also involved in spiritual searches and studies with a broad range of teachers and traditions. The story of that searching and of some of its findings can be found in the book noted below: Awake – Conscious Pilgrimage.

I've also loved writing and editing – mostly with and for a number of body-mind-spirit teachers – and cofounded a small press Wellspring Publications Ltd., in London, which published just a few books in its short life. I'm presently preparing a brief commentary of my understanding of the essential message of Patanjali's Yoga Sutras, intending to express this in fresh clear language to benefit new interested readers who wish to explore it – and themselves – more deeply.

Publications *(own books – excludes articles and editorial work)*

England's Festivals – A Year of Seasons, Customs and Traditions – published privately in 1982 and a revision published 2012 online with Amazon as e-book and paperback.

Conscious Eating – An Invitation to Intuitive Nourishment, co-authored with Shaun de Warren – published 2021 online with Amazon as e-book and paperback

Awake - Conscious Pilgrimage - An Evolving Soul's Progress (Draft) by A Pilgrim – published 2017 online with Amazon as e-book and paperback.

Who Am I? An Exploration of Our Essential Nature – published 2022 online with Amazon as e-book and paperback.(the last 2 are also freely available to read on scribd.com)

Jed Linde

Applying to Mexico City College after receiving my A.A. at Pasadena City College was one of the smartest decisions I have made during this lifetime. One way of reviewing my life could be: *Before MCC, During MCC and Mexico*, and *After MCC*. The college and Mexico were an adventure for me, one that opened my brain and my heart to previously unknown dimensions, experiences, and vistas.

One of them, was my search for lodging just two months after arriving at MCC in August, 1959. Staying at school-sponsored, low-priced housing with a family in Colonia Roma, I was content—forty-four dollars a month for a room and two meals. Then, I heard about Cuajimalpa, where everything was much cheaper. (I wanted to stretch my savings.) After school or on weekends, I searched in the appealing rustic town, just a mile and half above the school. I found *nada*. Frustratingly, I walked the streets asking anyone, *"Hay casa que puedo rentar?"* pushing my minimal Spanish to its limits. More *nada*, but with a few humorous incidents, when a local resident would reply, *"No hablo ingles,"* and repeated it when I said in Spanish that I was speaking Spanish. Finally, venting my woes in class, a student, "Tim," laughed and said, "I have a house, do you want to share it? (Ten dollars rent.) Now, I was living in the "real" Mexico, and loving it.

At MCC, and in Cuajimalpa and Mexico, I met my beloved Mexican wife, Maria Esther (who, sadly, passed last Thanksgiving after 63 years of marriage), learned Spanish, majored in Psychology (graduated *summa cum laude*, December, 1960), encountered Buddhism (*Zen and Psychoanalysis*, D.T. Suzuki, Fromm, and De Martino), and discovered non-European cultures and lifestyles. Our daughter was born in 1961, and I worked at *The News* as a columnist (movie, theater and TV, with the paper's moniker, "Eric Lang"). Having spent eight years in the D.F., I returned (with my wife and daughter) to the U.S. during the summer of 1967 (the Olympics' preparations having turned the city into a traffic-jammed, polluted, systems challenged, respiratory nightmare).

Between 1968 and 1972, my wife and I co-edited *Maguey*, a bilingual journal, subtitled *A Bridge Between Worlds*. After nine years practicing with a San Francisco-based Buddhist group (Shunryu Suzuki, Roshi), we moved to Carmel Valley, CA. Soon after, I began a four-decades-long bilingual psychotherapist career in Salinas, CA, during which I completed a Master's degree and a Doctorate. I retired a decade ago.

My marriage, writings during retirement (*Uranium Mine and Other Stories*, which has an MCC-related story, and a yet-to-be-published memoir), hosting the MCC History site Joseph Quinn created, creating this book, staying in touch with my wife's family members, and the Facebook MCC group, all keep me aware of my years in Mexico (my wife and I returned for multiple visits), and the benefits and blessings I received there.

In short, my decision to attend MCC was a life-changer (for the utmost better).

Publications:

Uranium Mine and Other Stories; e-book and paperback at multiple booksellers: https://books2read.com/u/4NoQwG

Maguey, a bridge between worlds; bilingual journal, Jed Linde and Maria Esther Manni, Eds. 1968-1972. All issues freely available at Open Source: https://www.jstor.org/site/reveal-digital/independent-voices/maguey28455648/?so=item_title_str_asc

Mexico City College The History 1940-1963 and Beyond by Joseph M. Quinn; Jed Linde, Editor. Available in e-book and paperback at multiple booksellers: https://books2read.com/u/mvPQj6

Nancy Westfall de Gurrola

After a year of college in my native Iowa, my parents decided that I needed to see more of the world. Having studied French in high school I assumed it would be Paris or the French Riviera. But no—the plan was for my mother and me to drive to Mexico City for a summer course. Obviously, I protested that I didn't intend to spend the summer with my mother or riding on a burro or sitting under a cactus wearing a funny hat! I sulked about the trip, sure we would never survive the drive through the long hot desert and, as many friends in Iowa had told me, the "bandidos" might get us.

Despite my resistance, we left for Mexico City in June 1961 for what was to be a 2-day trek through the northern desert of Mexico. Somewhere between Matehuala and San Luis Potosí the car suddenly stopped. Mom lifted the hood of the car but had no clue what was wrong. Trailer trucks and cars whizzed by, but finally a man in a pickup stopped and offered to help the two non-Spanish-speaking "gringas."

He began to take out one piece of the engine, put it on the ground, then another and another. My mother leaned into the window of the car where I remained sitting sullenly, cursing my fate in the sizzling heat, and said worriedly, "He's going to dismantle the car, not know how to fix it and just leave us here!"

My mom, who spoke no Spanish, and our "good Samaritan," who spoke no English, engaged in animated sign language. Suddenly looking very nervous, she said to me, "I think what he has asked for are my panties! What should I do?" Still angry at being dragged on this trip, I replied that she should just give them to him.

She got in the car, slipped them off and gave them to him through the window. After more sign language she said, "He wants yours too! Maybe then he'll go away!" I complied.

But no, he didn't go away but proceeded to tear the underpants into strips and tie them together. Observing this, my mother cried, "God help us! He's going to strangle us with our own underwear!" Now I was frightened too!

Just as we were about to run down the road trying to escape, he began tinkering under the hood, replacing the parts of the engine that were strewn around. He signaled mom to try the ignition. The engine started! What had been a very scary moment suddenly turned into a humorous incident. He had fashioned a fan belt out of our underwear! We then followed him to a mechanic's shop in San Luis Potosí to get proper repairs.

Why hadn't our "good Samaritan" asked for a blouse or a handkerchief? He had needed something that would stretch! (We heard later that besides ladies' underwear, pantyhose could be used as a fan belt but pantyhose had not been readily available until the mid-1960s and who would have worn them in the desert anyway?!)

Moral of the story? My stereotypes of Mexico disappeared forever! The exceptional helpfulness and ingenuity of our clever "guardian angel" inspired me to want to know more about Mexico and its people.

Editor's Note: The essay above won a "My Mexico Moment" contest and was published in the April 28, 2022 issue of The Eye, a monthly all-English magazine that focuses on Mexico. It is available online at: https://theeyehuatulco.com/

Memoir

I arrived to Mexico in the summer of 1961 for a six-week course at Mexico City College but was so intrigued and curious about the country that I decided first to stay for the fall semester, then to transfer from Iowa State University. I graduated *cum laude* in 1963 with a degree in Latin American Studies. MCC by then had become the University of the Americas. My mentor for these years was Dr. Richard Greenleaf, who asked me to teach several courses starting in 1965.

While studying for my master's degree, I was Editor of *The Collegian*. I received my MA in Latin American History in 1967. I continued to teach and became a full professor in 1970 when I moved with the University of the Americas when it relocated to Cholula, Puebla.

I returned to Mexico City and in 1977 joined the faculty of the Universidad Iberoamericana where I continued to teach as well as coordinate the program for foreign students. Between 1970 and 1985 I was visiting lecturer five times at Tulane University in New Orleans, where I spent my sabbatical in 1994.

Through the Universidad Iberoamericana and the University of North Carolina's Center for International Understanding, I coordinated a unique program designed to build networks of state and local educators and leaders in North Carolina and Mexico to address challenges raised by that state's rapid growth of immigration. In 2002, Gov. Michael Easley honored me to be the recipient of *The Order of the Long Leaf Pine*, "for exemplary service to North Carolina."

Although I retired from my administrative position at the University in 1999, I continued to teach and coordinate special programs until I reluctantly retired in 2015, after 50 years of a rewarding career teaching Mexican history and Mexico-U.S. Relations to students from every continent!

I am a member Alpha Delta Kappa, the international professional honorary organization for women educators, and served as National President of ADK in Mexico from 2000 – 2002. In July 2001 I was invited to address the ADK International Convention in Boston on the topic of the Mexican Education System.

While a student I met Juan Ramon Gurrola. We dated for four years and were married in December 1965 when he graduated as an architect. We enjoyed traveling to all 31 states of Mexico as well as to China, much of Europe, Central and South America, and the Caribbean. Our three children were born and raised in Mexico and we have five grandchildren. My husband passed away in 2021.

I never would have imagined that my life in Mexico would be so full—living in one of the world's largest cities is challenging but also very stimulating and rewarding. Just one example: I have had the privilege of meeting several Nobel Peace prize recipients (Mikhail Gorbachev, Norman Borlaug, and Rigoberta Manchu) when they visited Mexico. And our dear friend, Ricardo Zapata, was a member of the U.N.'s Intergovernmental Panel on Climate Change that shared the Nobel Peace Prize with Al Gore in 2007. Never would have happened had I stayed in my hometown of Boone, Iowa!!

I have witnessed many positive and some not so positive events and changes since 1961. Through it all Mexico has remained resilient, hopeful and optimistic about the future.

Viva Mexico!

Sandra Moe

Thought I'd try to sum up my memories of MCC before they ALL disappear.

It was 1961, when I left Minnesota and took a bus to Mexico City to my housing in Anzures, and it was 1971, when I left MCC as it was moving to Puebla.

I received my BA in Spanish in 1964, and in 1969, a *cum laude* Bachelor of Arts in Psychology, followed the next year with a Master's degree in Psychology. I also did a freshman year at Moorhead, Minnesota and received an Honorable Mention. I love to learn, and basically that is what I am constantly doing, so identify as a life-long learner.

My first years in Mexico were filled with explorations: traveling to the Yucatan in the early days of only Coca Cola signs, dubious mo/hotels but good company in a Volkswagen car; never drank pulque after first taste, but got well acquainted with tequila brands at Garibaldi Square; ate any offered foods such as beetles and came to prefer *tacos al pastor*; was part of a study group on Marxism; met, married and divorced the father of my son; remember where I was when the Bay of Pigs was invaded, JFK was shot, the Kent State Massacre, and numerous happenings in Mexico because I still follow news there: Chiapas, crime and cartels as of recent days.

I needed to work, and by 1966 was the administrative assistant (secretary) to President Lindley, so I was aware of the school's educational, financial and political "issues" until 1971. In 1970, I was appointed Dean for Women and paid less than the subsequent Men's Dean, who had less Spanish but more money.

In my short time as Dean, I was often involved with the *policia,* and with embassies regarding students who had accidents or were arrested. One involved students living in Cuajimalpa, who had lots of marijuana in their house when the *policia* arrived. I visited students in prison and in hospitals, and at times was the translator between the parents and the officials. Parents would sometimes call, and while these were adult students it was usually helpful if some communication was available to them—it was the end of the 60's and start of the 70's.

In September 1971, I immigrated to Canada and was a research assistant at UBC in psychology, subsequently with UBC Health Science Center doing research on the effectiveness of therapies; I also taught Spanish at Simon Fraser University for a semester. From 1973 to 1974 I worked providing assessments and therapy to children in government care. The times were changing however and I imagine that many of us in the 70's came to new realizations as the two English speaking countries to the north began talking about racism, sexism, gender and other topics that have been unearthed since those days. I was working at CAS during a time when many had not yet acknowledged what became known as the "60's scoop of indigenous children". Domestic violence had yet to be labeled as such.

In 1974, I started working at what is now Capilano University in North Vancouver. For the next 26 years I laboured in the field of psychology developing courses such as Psychology of Adolescence, Psychology of Aging, Psychology of Women and working to develop a Department of Women's Studies - now Gender Studies. The years have blended but I enjoyed my career. I also taught English in Yantai, China; in Havana, Cuba and had a Women's Studies course one semester at the Iberoamericana. I traveled to the Ukraine in the 1980's on an education course as I was also studying at either SFU in gerontology or at

UBC in various courses.

My years in Mexico were very formative in how I experience the world and in what I did with my life. After I first retired in 2000, I volunteered with the Latin American Writers Festival and other groups needing helpers. I slowed down in 2017, and, of course, we all know/remember what happened in 2020 (Covid). I'm delighted that I still have friends in Mexico and in other countries.

Todd Tarbox

September 22, 1964/Tuesday

Mexico City, Mexico

I arrived in Mexico City last night just past the bewitching hour, weary but exhilarated at the prospect of starting a new chapter. You genuinely appreciate travel and distance aboard a train. The vast geographic and social contrasts between the Land of Lincoln and the Halls of Montezuma are quite educational.

First impressions: What disparities there are down here! Walking down a broad and beautiful main drag last night, Avenida Reforma (reported to be one of the most expansive and stately boulevards in the world), which seems to consist of nothing but silver shops, banks, and assorted *tiendas por los ricos*, I almost stepped on an elderly gentleman in rags, asleep in the middle of the sidewalk, tucked in the fetal position, with assorted empty cerveza bottles forming a nimbus over his head. He was so disheveled that you couldn't quite tell where his beard ended and his rags began. Humanity scurried and ambled around and over him. He was ignored—avoided as if he were some unspeakable piece of offal. I appeared to be the only one who noticed this dispossessed soul. Though, like the rest of humanity that scuttled by, I didn't do anything to help and walked away.

What do you do? Maybe I'll find out in time.

September 23, 1964

San Francisco Hotel, Luis Moya 11, Mexico 1, D.F.

I arrived at mid-afternoon yesterday at Sra. Rodriqueses' casa in Colonia Lomas de Chapultepec, just in time to meet a fellow student who had arrived moments before by plane. The ostentatious wealth displayed in Lomas rivals, if not exceeds, Chicago's Gold Coast. Block-long, walled estates are not uncommon. So that the sensibilities of the Lomasites are not disturbed, a sixteen-foot wall, topped with broken glass embedded in concrete, separates this exclusive conclave from the rabble. On the other side of this wall, which stretches for many blocks, is a deep *barranca* (ravine) home to a teeming sea of humanity who comprise the "other half." Here, human wrecks live in crowded, cacophonous squalor, the likes of which I have never seen (no running water, no plumbing, no hope—street scenes that would make Dickens and Hogarth blush). Nondescript doors are located along this wall at intervals of several blocks, which allow entrance and egress to the residents of this Latin Lower Depths, allowing the denizens the privilege to cross the street and break their asses as they do the bidding of their well-heeled neighbors.

Back to Casa Rodriguez. Appearances can be, and often are, deceiving. Upon entering, I was impressed by the expansive, handsomely appointed first floor. However, the higher we climbed, the seedier the accommodations. Elegant paneling on the first floor, peeling plaster on the second floor, and more lath than crumbling plaster on the third-floor room to which I was directed. The accommodations are so devoid of charm, not to mention promise, that I told her I would pay only by the day and hoped to be away shortly.

Let me describe the school before I tell you about the housing situation. It's sixteen kilometers from the heart of Mexico City, a couple of thousand feet above Mexico City, just off the highway from Mexico City to Toluca (Carretera Mexico-Toluca). This four-lane free-for-all is never void of heavy traffic. The campus is tiny. A half dozen cottages nestled together comprise the business and faculty offices, the dean's quarters, and assorted student organizations. The school is comprised of a slightly more extensive collection of cottages. Between these two architectural clusters looms the most prominent building, which houses a theatre, additional classrooms, and offices. Abutting this building is an expansive patio providing a spectacular view of Mexico City.

The University has a fleet of dilapidated buses, which shuttle students and faculty to and from Mexico City from seven in the morning until four in the afternoon. No school shuttle runs from the school to points west (toward Toluca), where I plan to live. However, transportation to and from school should be no problem, for there is a constant stream of buses traversing between Toluca and Mexico City, and with a wave of an arm, the driver will stop and pick you up. Unlike most U.S. bus lines of my acquaintance, which provide customers with one "grade" of service, Mexico provides travelers with a rich assortment of bus options, from 1st to 4th class. The last class passengers are comprised of the dispossessed, the impoverished, livestock of every description, and your son. At one peso a ride (.08 cents), it's the best travel buy I've come across. From the campus to the little village, El Contadero, which I hope to call home, is a steady climb of several thousand feet.

Interestingly, this 20th-century road accommodates motorists traveling more than 70 mph and rag pickers in push carts leisurely strolling at three miles an hour. I'm told accidents are frequent, and near-misses are constant. Travel certainly does broaden.

This afternoon, I will look at a cottage in El Contadero that a graduate student is renting and is looking for someone to share the rent.

I have decided on English as a major. For the first quarter, I'm enrolled in Spanish, History of Civilization, Creative Writing (poetry writing), and 19th Century English Literature. I'm a little overwhelmed, but I'm convinced that coming to Mexico to experience another culture makes sense.

September 27, 1964

El Contadero, Mexico

The casa in El Contadero is perfect. It's west of the campus and approximately two thousand feet higher. The views to the east are spectacular.

Contadero, I discovered, means "a passage where only one person can pass at a time," an apt metaphor for life, no? This cottage is part of a compound of four dwellings owned by a film salesman who lives in Mexico City. My share of the rent is 400 pesos ($32.00) a month. A maid comes with the place, and we each pay her 100 pesos a month ($8.00). Food, I'm told, never exceeds 300 pesos ($24.00) a month. Bottled water, gas, and electricity amount to something less than 50 pesos ($4.00) a month. So, living should come to about 850 pesos (or $68.00 a month).

I have never seen the likes of where I'll be living. It's a two-story adobe bungalow with whitewashed walls on the first floor. In my digs, the loft twigs are embedded in the adobe walls, which add a rustic touch. The ceiling has ten beams supporting twice as many cross pieces, supporting interior wooden shingles. At the roof's peak, I'm able to stand. Anyone over 5'10" living up here would risk developing a permanent stoop. Aside from several gaping holes running along the apex (which I've stuffed with rags), I'm entirely charmed with my living arrangement.

Without a car, I'm doing the city a service by not adding to the Federal District (Mexico City) motorized mayhem, where drivers, particularly macho males, engage in automotive anarchy in a highly stylized and animated dance of death. Madness!

September 27, 1964

108

El Contadero, Mexico

It is on the far side of 6:30 p.m. on this lofty mountainside. The sun is setting, and from off to my left, three blocks from our modest compound, the cacophonous whine of incessant traffic scampering up and down the pike to and from Mexico City is somewhat muted by the nearby leaves blowing in the early-evening breeze. To make a phone call from El Contadero to Mexico City, some fifteen miles, costs 10 pesos for ten minutes, so you can picture the tab for a call to Mt. Morris!

A fellow student pulled in last night from La Jolla, California, to finish up his work toward a B.A. in Anthropology. He's proficient in French, Spanish, and a smattering of German. He's a bright, genuine, and engaging sort. This afternoon, he, two maids that work in the compound, two children of the eldest maid, and I went to a park about ten kilometers west of here. The scenery was breathtaking, ten thousand feet above sea level, wandering through 100-foot, arrow-straight pine trees. The higher you climb, the deeper the forest. Amid this sylvan wilderness, we turned a corner, and our eyes were assaulted by the sight of a mud hut with a faded and chipped "Orange Crush Drink" sign covering the entire front of the structure. There was a dismal beauty to the squalor; in addition to selling Orange Crush, this family, comprised of one adult female merchant and six infant merchants, hawked straw creations spread over every inch of free dirt in the front of their modest crumbling adobe home. Not in the market for straw kitsch, we got back in the car. We headed further into the mountains, arriving moments later at a 17th-century monastery, Desierto de los Leones, nestled in the forest. This former way station to the True Cross is now a national park. What a mighty fortress ecclesiastics fashioned. The centuries have softened the place. Pulque, beer, and fire-hot tamales hawked by the cheerful vendors of disparate ages have replaced the padres proffering wine and wafers. Today's raucous, fun-seeking day-trippers and ardent canoodling young couples have supplanted yesterday's pious supplicants. Progress?

Returning, I strolled through El Contadero. A gringo is viewed as something exotic in this sleepy little village. If not exotic, I certainly stick out. I'm happy to report that all my encounters with the denizens of this village are exceedingly friendly. I smile my way through town, and when I attempt the most rudimentary Spanish, my audience is remarkably patient and appreciative.

El Contadero is on the left side of the highway heading away from Mexico City (as is the University); when I had sufficiently run out of storefronts to peek into and faces to smile at, I crossed to the other side of the Mexico City-Toluca highway to investigate the village of Cuajimalpa, with its serpentine main drag that parallels the highway. Cuajimalpa appears to be a bit more prosperous and larger than El Contadero. Its downtown consists of tiny, one-room tiendas (stores) that offer an eclectic assortment of merchandise, from an abattoir to a button and fabric emporium. A flower-bedecked park in the center of town is a logical gathering place. Young lovers, old lovers, children, with and without parents, the poor, and the not-so-poor gather around a fountain, enjoying one another's company. School begins on Tuesday.

October 2, 1964

El Contadero, Mexico

The first week has ended, and it is time for reflection—or at least it should be. The hour is late, and I am too weak to write.

I've begun to bump into some bright and entertaining characters, both students and faculty. The university population is genuinely global; half the students are fellow gringos, thirty percent are nationals, and the remaining twenty percent are from Europe, Asia, and Latin America.

October 14, 1964

El Contadero, Mexico

Occasionally, I ask myself what I am doing in Mexico. Did I come to Mexico to run from responsibility or seek it out? Life is one endless question. Why Mexico City? Why study so far away? What is success? What is failure? What's the point of anything/everything?

What about my classes? Spanish is necessary and a requirement. Western Civilization is a challenge. It's taught by a very bright, humorless chain smoker. Between incessant cigarette, he says much that's worth attending. English 202 (literature) is a delight, and Poetry 329 is the high point of my day. A superb professor, who, in appearance, reminds me of Robert Frost, teaches the class. In his youth, he considered becoming a Trappist Monk, but he was deemed too frail, and for years, he was a writer and an editor in New York. He co-edited a collection of pieces about the Virgin of Guadalupe, *The Dark Virgin: The Book of Our Lady of Guadalupe.* As a pre-teen in Connecticut, he had the great fortune of benefiting from the sage advice and humor of his neighbor, Mark

Twain. Years later, he wrote a thin volume on his childhood hero. A decade ago, he moved to Mexico to teach and continue writing. A bachelor, he recently adopted two infant Mexican foundlings—a brilliant and charming fellow, he.

October 22, 1964

El Contadero, Mexico

It's a quiet Thursday evening. The tinkling and bubbling of the water tank keep me company and help blot out the early evening sounds of children shouting, dogs whining, and gears grinding on the steady procession of vehicles scurrying to and from Mexico City and Toluca. An oversized gas heater palpitates and murmurs at my feet, and a rim-chipped cup with Lipton Tea simmers on the desk to my left. The tea, I might add, was left by the previous renter, George, who departed the country in haste and in medias res late this summer after having had the good fortune to write a check for eight pesos and mistakenly received from his bank eight thousand pesos. George, as I understand, didn't feel particularly compelled to acknowledge the error and decided to make a quick exit north. In his flight, George left all that he had acquired over the past year while taking a few courses in the "fine arts" at the university. Many of his not-so-full "fine arts," including a series of crudely drawn self-portraits reminiscent of Ray Milland in "Lost Weekend." In addition to his objects d'art, he left a large lump of soiled blue jeans, ragged sweatshirts, and assorted other unidentifiable I need to burn.

I understand that George suffered from a nervous disorder that caused him to lose much of his motor control, shake, and often drop whatever he might be holding, which manifested itself during moments of stress and was further exacerbated when he tippled demon rum. In this condition, he would slam instead of closing doors, bang into furniture rather, and navigate through a room that resulted in countless broken doors, windows, plates, and glasses.

The chips and rends he left us to add a certain panache to this askew cottage and my world, which, too, is slightly aslant. The only major challenge he left was a smashed toilet, which necessitated our use of the neighbor's john. Until coming up here, I always took a toilet for granted. No longer. We have called a plumber and are confident he will arrive sometime before I graduate.

I'm getting used to the near-freezing water in the shower (but grateful there's running water; it's a luxury in this village).

October 29, 1964

El Contadero, Mexico

Not a few students I've met here maintain an attitude of, "Down here, so what the hell? I'm two thousand miles from home, and nobody will ever know what I'm doing." I remain on the periphery, content to observe the asininity around me rather than to be a part of it. This is neither good nor bad, but just me.

After multiple trips to various governmental offices to receive official approval to study in this country, today, I finally filled in my last form. I had it properly stamped in quadruplet by a legion of scowling government functionaries, shuffling about in drab olive green offices, attired in drab olive green uniforms. It's taken so long, a professor told me, because I didn't grease anyone's palms. The custom of paying off officials with a "propina" (tip)/"mordida" (bite, i.e., illegal payment) is endemic in Mexico. Pay the mordida, and you receive services. Don't proffer a propina or mordida; you can wait and wait until Hell freezes. Once the freeze thaws, these guys will still be around waiting with their hands out. Yes, the "payoff" is universal; in the U.S., it is perhaps more subtle. Down here, it's a flourishing way of life. I've witnessed another example of this practice: an army of retainers who "watch" your parked car. If you don't pay them something before departing, you may return to discover a damaged or missing car. When someone pumps gas into your car, you are expected to tip him; if you don't, you may not drive away very easily. Bureaucracies, rubber stamps, and heavy hands are everywhere! It doesn't just keep the economy going—it is the economy!

November 23, 1964

El Contadero, Mexico

A copy of *A Shropshire Lad* is on my left. It's a reflective night: "... Oh never fear, man naughty's to dread, /Look not left nor right:/In all the endless road you tread/There's nothing but the night."

Last Friday, classes were suspended due to "Dia de la Revolucion," this break—the third such holiday suspension this quarter—allowed me to confine myself to my garret and study. I read Hardy's *The Return of the Native,* an ambling and penetrating look into 19th Century Wessex country, with the locals vibrating frustrations, traumas, breaches of faith, and losses.

Here's a little news: the presidential election—it seemed to me, from this southerly vantage point, that politics shot for and hit a new low. Frankly, I wouldn't care to buy a used car from either of the two standard-bearers! But there's always Bobby Kennedy, with his "lean and hungry" look (who showed up here last week to open a vast low-cost housing complex named for his brother) in the wings for '68.

The only notable reverberation of the election is that I am out five pesos to my roommate. I wagered that Goldwater wouldn't pick up twenty percent of the popular vote.

Closer to my mountain top, the Mexican elections are on the horizon, making it an exceptionally festive time for members of the dominating (actually, it's the only serious) political party. I wonder why they go through the charade of elections. The outcome is known the moment the "candidate" is nominated. The election process is indicative of the way much of this country operates. The word defining how this country is "run" isn't democracy, liberty, or freedom. The word is power, the word is obedience to that power, and the word is rampant patronage. You aren't encouraged to question in this culture. Equally disturbing is the legal system down here, based on the Napoleonic Code, which proclaims that if you are arrested, you are guilty until proven innocent (or you succumb to paying a mordida).

I just purchased a chicken. It all started innocently enough. On one of my many walks through my hamlet, I came across a chicken farm about three blocks east of us, next door to the local Casa de Pulque" (about which I will have more to say in a moment). It was like Toad of Toad Hall encountering his first motor car. I had to have a chicken. With much animation and a leave of my senses, I walked away with one mighty fine hen for thirty pesos. Now, two weeks later, with mountains of feed pecked away and with only a handful of eggs in my basket, I'm debating whether the bird is fat enough to eat or whether the fried eggs in themselves are a sufficient reward to send me into poverty. A considerable dilemma is this. Have you ever had a freshly laid egg? I mean, an egg that has just dropped into your hand, so fresh that it serves as a hand warmer. I had my first such experience this afternoon upon returning from school. I want to expound on the exquisite difference in taste between a homegrown, warm-to-the-touch egg and a store-bought egg of indeterminate age. But I'm damned if I can tell the difference.

The other day, I met my housemate's novia. The poor (in every sense of the word) girl's domestic arrangement is heart-rending. She lives in a one-bedroom apartment (hovel) in the heart of Mexico City that includes a kitchen consisting of a broken and begrimed stove and sink, sans running water, which she shares with six other dispossessed souls. None, she told us, were relatives but just fellow transients who, by day, forage on the streets to stay alive and, by night, huddle in these grim quarters to muster the courage and strength to confront another day scratching for a few pesos on the teeming, gritty streets in the nation's capital. Entering this despair was like walking into the second act of Gorky's *Lower Depths*. I saw two other young girls sleeping on one bed with a soiled plastic sheet that was ill-serving as a blanket. To their right, an affable night watchman, Salvador, was preparing to go to work. A duck and a string of five ducklings marched over an old wraith, sleeping soundly on another bed. Until I witnessed this disturbing scene, I suspected that Oscar Lewis' examination of Mexico City's underclass, *The Children of Sanchez,* was possibly an overwrought account. This visit disabused me of any such thought.

Their living arrangement is anything but unique. I'm told tens of thousands of such living arrangements are throughout the city. It was an astonishing site for a country boy from the rolling plains of Ogle County, Illinois.

I try to juxtapose high culture with low. Last week, I attended an excellent production of Ionesco's *The Bald Soprano* at "Casa del Lago" (House on the Lake), a converted drawing room of a spectacular mansion on the city's west side. Ionesco has a cast of characters who spend an "absurd" several hours struggling to communicate with each other and make sense of the ambiguous present.

My housemate fancies himself an entrepreneur. The other day, he and I took a trip to the Toluca market to check into the possibility of his exporting sweaters. Seeing little there, we headed to Metepec, a few miles away. It was a Monday, and Monday is traditionally market day. The enclosed photo is the exterior of a pottery shop dealing exclusively in clay pots and clay Virgin Marys—a perfect metaphor for much of the Mexican landscape: utility and divinity. As for my housemate's exporting dream, after much-animated negotiating, he bought a sweater for himself. This is a start. Maybe next week, he'll buy a second sweater and get serious! If nothing comes of it, at least he'll stay warm this winter. I just spotted a rat the size of the sink scurry through the kitchen, only to meet its fate in the claws and fangs of George's cat. "Life is real; life is earnest," to quote Henry Wadsworth Longfellow.

Todd's Postscript:

I entered Mexico for the first time in the fall of 1964 and enrolled at UA, graduating from that magical multicultural universe three years later with a dual English and Creative Writing degree.

In recent months, I've begun cobbling together a book comprised of letters (a selection of them preceded this note) between me and my artist father, Hascy, with a working title: *Man Does Not Live on Junk Mail Alone/A Life of Letters Between a Father and Son.*

Throughout my years at UA, I spent many fruitful days outside the classroom exploring and absorbing the myriad lessons Mexico has to teach—good and ill—and while doing so, I captured many of my learning experiences on film. Many were displayed at a photo exhibit ("Young Mexico") on campus and published in the *Mexico Quarterly Review,* shortly before I graduated. (Several of them follow this note.)

The January 28, 1968 Collegian review stated, "Todd Tarbox's moving photographs are designed to give a glimpse into the heart of Mexican life. Tarbox's one-man show at the university last year established him as a photographer of sensitivity and realism, vitally interested in people and human problems in today's world."

https://catarina.udlap.mx/ximg/db/xmlibris/
sala_de_archivos_y_colecciones_especiales/fondo_moderno/
periodicos_universitarios/volumen_20/1967_02_24.pdf

My "sensitivity, realism, and vital interest in people and human problems in today's world" then and now were enhanced immeasurably by my years in Mexico and at the University of the Americas.

AL
BENEMERITO
BENITO JUAREZ
LA PATRIA
MEXICO QUARTERLY REVIEW
Vol. 2 No.
FALL 1967

Corona
EXT
LA CERVEZ

Geof Schwer

I attended MCC/UA from Winter '62 through Summer '64, when I matriculated with a BBA in International Business. I returned to Austin and did my graduate work at UT. In 1964, I received a Master's degree in International Finance.

My first job was with Brown & Root in Houston. Every week I would make out reimbursement checks for foreign projects in the amount of $500K-$750K and mail them off without even a co-signer! I left B&R in '66 and went to work for Dean Van Lines, where I handled all its military shipments into and out of the port of Houston, including documenting, invoicing and clearing US Customs. On one of my last trips to Customs, I saw a Ferrari engine loaded on to a non-descript pickup truck and driven away. That was kind of questionable, but not nearly as much as when the Customs Inspector told me to mark it as "Lost in Transit"!

I finally ended up in Waco, Texas, where my computer skills using UNIX and the earliest versions of DOS lead me to Texas State Technical Institute (then James Connolly Technical Institute). I worked there until my retirement 38 years later.

I never got to work in international business in Latin America, but I still had a very productive and interesting life.

Nor do I regret one moment of my experience at MCC/UA. I am sure it has helped me in many untold ways.

I enjoy retirement by rebuilding a '91 Corvette and playing the tenor sax (for my own enjoyment).

Larry Mottice

I attended Mexico City College the winter quarter of 1960, along with some other Ohio State students. Great experience.

Several of us responded to an advertisement looking for extras in the filming of a movie. Turned out we were hired for the filming of "The Magnificent Seven. " Yul Brynner and Steve McQueen. A small village was built for the film outside Mexico City. . .We got paid, and had to cut classes for a few days, but it was worth it.

We would hitchhike to Acapulco on weekends. You could see Mt. Popo while eating lunch on the college terrace between classes. Paseo de la Reforma and un peso taxis were the big thing. The peso was worth 8 cents at the time. You could buy a beer for 1 peso. Train trip to Vera Cruz for Mardi Gras was scary.

I finished my education at OSU

Many great memories, and I learned to be very fond of the Mexican people.

Bill Dean

I went to visit a friend who was a student at the UDLA in Mexico City for the first time during Spring Break in 1967. I was from a small mill town in Green Bay, WI where the highest thing was a paper mill smoke stack and I had been attending college in WIS. That was a game changer for me as I immediately fell head over heels for Mexico City and the UDLA Toluca Highway campus.

I returned that winter of 1968 as a full-time student and lived in Polanco in the Capital until winter of 1970 when I moved to Berkeley California for 2 years and returned to finish my degree at the new Cholula UDLAP campus where I graduated in 1973 with a B.A. in History.

Living in Mexico City was amazing with the endless opportunities to experience Mexican culture, enjoy great weather, watch in detail the political life around the 1968 Olympics, know about our Embassy, escape on weekends to Cuernavaca & Acapulco, and visit the pyramids at Teotihuacan. There was never a dull moment living in the DF, as we called it then. Life in the BIG CITY was never boring!

Originally, I was against the move from the highway campus to Cholula, a location which was void of the life Mexico City had and lacking nearly everything I had gotten used to in the Capital. When I first got there moving back to Mexico from Berkeley, in the Fall of 1972, it was a shock. I found myself often taking the 3rd class bus back to Mexico City many weekends to escape the cornfields that surrounded the UDLAP campus.

But then...I found Cholula & San Andres to be interesting and even liked Puebla. I felt I really got to see another facet of Mexico that one could never get living in Polanco where I was in the DF. Life in Cholula was simple and cheap too and I first stayed in a dorm on the campus. I even once lived in a Mexican family's farm rental room which cost me $13 a month! I had a view of Popo from my 2nd floor room.

Later I moved to what was a guest house inside one of the few villas in Cholula, which was almost next to the great Cholula pyramid. I became very interested in Meso-American history and Cholula was a great place to be for that topic.

I also met an incredible group of fellow students both in the DF & at Cholula. Moreover, the UDLA faculty was outstanding at both locations.

To this day, I credit the luck I had to experience life in another culture, enjoy topics I would never have experienced in the USA and credit that experience with helping me become a successful and happy person to this day.

I still go to Mexico most winters, where I often live in San Miguel de Allende and I always go back to Mexico City...it is always fun to visit.

Ricardo Cassin

Post-MCC history ... Feb. 2008

Compañeros,

I've been lurking on the site for several months now, and although my time at MCC overlapped many of you, I don't think - or remember -having met any of you. That's amazing, given how small MCC was in those days.

.

I was at MCC fulltime (4 quarters each year) from 1959 through the end of Summer Quarter of 1962, when I graduated with a B.A. in International Relations and Economics. Originally from Santa Fe, New Mexico, my mother's family was from Mexico City, and I was sent off for high school there, where I attended the Instituto Iberoamericano, and lived in La Lomas (on Palmas) with my aunt, uncle, and cousins. My mother felt that the "sharp edges" of New Mexico were starting to show through, and so I was shipped off to be "mexicanizado" - or civilized, as my mother would say. My New Mexican Spanish particularly offended her, even though it was my first language, and we spoke Spanish at home (my father was a local "New" Mexican). As many of you have expressed before me, my experience - and education - at MCC were formative in almost every sense. Even after 46 years, I count my time in Mexico City and at MCC to be among the most memorable times of my life, and I think we were in Mexico City during its best times. A pleasant, civil, safe, livable small city of only 5 million, where you could walk almost anywhere at any time of the day or night without ever having to look over your shoulder.

The people I particularly remember were Pat Macaulay, Mel Dethlefs, John Sevier, the gorgeous Victoria Verringer, Robert Vallejo, Walter Hulse, Paco Longoria, David Money, Joe Houchin, Cordley Coit, Carl Swann, Marcella Slezack, Armando Gomez-Palacios, Larry Close, Diana Ontiveros, Lidia Sotomayor (who married a Canadian named Stan). Other names will come back as I try to reconnect the neurons, and there are many others whose first names and faces I remember, but who's last names escape me.

MCC was interesting socially during my time there, and lasting friendships formed among those who were there for the long haul ... to actually get a degree. The GI Bill guys were older by nearly a decade, and with a few exceptions, had little interest in socializing with us "kids". Interestingly, there wasn't a lot of interaction between the Americans and the relatively few local Mexican students, most of whom -like myself - were "niños bien" from well-to-do Chilango families. At this point, the locals had not really discovered MCC, and because all classes were in English, only those who already spoke English well felt comfortable at MCC. I think that my circle of friends was unusual, because it included both Gringos and local Mexicans. A lot of us were dating local girls, and quite a few oof the American girls had Mexican -or European - boyfriends. It was an interestingly sophisticated group for our relatively young age, most of which came from some money both in the U.S. and Mexico, and almost all of us had spent some time in Europe. After 8 years in Mexico (5 years at the Ibero, and 3 at MCC) my mother was finally satisfied that the rough edges of New Mexico in my character had been honed reasonably smooth, and I was finally able to speak Spanish without "gringoismos" or the 18th century vocabulary of New Mexican Spanish. I still sometimes relapse, however.

The faculty I remember best were Richard Greenleaf, John Savage, Fernando Horcasitas, Luis Zorrilla, Sra. Rivas, Toby Joysmith. Again ... there are a lot of faces I can still see, but can't yet put names to.

Anyhow, I wonder if any of THIS group might remember me or any of the friends I mentioned above? I seem to be 3-4 years younger than most of you.

After finishing up at MCC in 1962 I spent almost three years in Europe, two years in Rome and a year in Geneva, working some odd jobs, teaching Spanish and English, ski-bumming, doing some freelance writing, and trying to stay off the family dole without putting too much of a crimp in my fulltime girl-chasing. My uncle was Mexican ambassador to Italy while I was there, so needless to say, life was pretty good.

I went back to New Mexico in 1965, and got into the Ph.D. program in History at the University of New Mexico - a primo program at the time, and I was able to keep life and limb together by teaching at the Peace Corps Training Center for Latin America which was at UNM. I finished classwork, and got started on a doctoral dissertation, but in 1969money was getting thin (minimal support for grad students there) and my wife-at-the-time and I decided that it was time to escape New Mexico for San Francisco before all of the flower children went extinct. We eventually got a divorce and went our own ways. I had some moderate success as a freelance writer, and ended up working for the San Francisco Chronicle, writing rock music reviews with John Wasserman, the Chron's entertainment editor.

That was enormous fun, and I got to spend the best part of the 70s in the psycho-sexual paradise of the Northern California music scene, living on my 36' Tahiti Ketch in Sausalito. In March of 1975 I decided that the South Pacific called, so after some provisioning and other

preparations, singlehanded, I sailed out under the Golden Gate Bridge and turned left. After a 4- month trip down the Mexican coast and ultimately to the Galapagos and the Marquesas, my downhill run to Papeete concluded in Tahiti, where I was to spend more than a year exploring Tahiti, Bora Bora, Huahine, and the other Society Islands, and the wonders of Tahitian girls. After about a year, I figured that I might have two years of money left, so I decided to complete my circumnavigation of the South Pacific, and start heading home. Leaving Tahiti, I headed west through the Cook Islands and Tonga to Pago Pago in American Samoa, the absolute turnaround point on the trip. I had thought seriously of doing a complete circumnavigation of the globe, but figured I didn't have enough money, so after provisioning and some deferred maintenance, I headed north through the Line Islands (Suvarov, Christmas, etc.) and came into Hawaii the back way ... a real pisser of an upwind sail. After a couple of weeks of rest in Hawaii, I started off on the last leg back to San Francisco ... which took me 4 grueling upwind-sailing weeks. By that time, the old Golden Gate looked like the gates of heaven. Home.

I arrived with about $1,000 in traveler's checks, and $2,000 still in my San Francisco checking account. Miraculously, the S.F. Chronicle immediately gave me my old job back part-time, and I actually rented an apartment, after having lived for 6 years on the old "Albatross". The following Fall I entered the Master's program in Biology at San Francisco State, and to make a long story a little shorter, ultimately entered the Ph.D. program at Stanford, which I finished in 1984. After Stanford I came down here to La Jolla to do a postdoc at Scripps Institution of Oceanography in Biological Oceanography. I went from Scripps to the Ocean Sciences Research Institute, where I was Executive Director for about 20 years until I retired in 2006.

I'm still peripherally involved in the oceanography academic community, but I'm finished with research. My wife Lynn and I still live in La Jolla, in the hills overlooking the Scripps Oceanography campus and the Pacific. We're fortunately still in great health, and religiously run 3-5 miles on the beach most days, and surf 2-3 times each week.

Currently - and for the past year - I've been working on a historical novel set in Morelos at the beginning of the Revolution of 1910, where my mother's family were sugar planters and deeply involved in events of the day. I have a great literary agent who has generated some publisher interest in the book, so it seems likely that it will eventually be published. All I have to do is finish it.

So that's MY post-MCC story. Over the years I've followed the development of the Universidad de las Américas, Puebla, and have visited the impressive Cholula campus several times. Some of my nieces and nephews have happily gone to school there, and received superb educations. Until the recent regime, it has been an excellent university ... perhaps the best private school in Mexico ... and it's sad to see that it has fallen on hard times due to human folly. I

sincerely hope that they are able to recover. The Universidad de las Américas in Mexico City is an interesting contrast. It too is impressive in its own way, with something like 5,000 students. It has an excellent reputation, and is focused on the humanities and social sciences, not unlike the early MCC model. Unlike the Puebla institution, it is very "urban", and has the feel of a small NYU with a Mexican accent. I have visited it several times, and found both faculty and administrators to be cordial and highly competent. Two of my cousin's children received their degrees there, and went on to good Ph.D. programs in the U.S. Both institutions - although very different -are heir to the MCC history and tradition, and are worthy of our support.

Anyhow ... I would be most interested in hearing about the post-MCC histories of OTHER members of the group, and I sincerely hope that they will be forthcoming.

Un cordial saludo a todos, Ricardo Cassín, Ph.D. La Jolla, California

Editor's Note: This fascinating memoir, sent to Joseph Quinn sixteen years ago, was for the MCC History site, or to be posted on the (now

closed) Yahoo group, but was not utilized at the time. Thank you, Ricardo, for a great memoir. Jed Linde, 2024

Obituary

Dr. Richard Cassin passed away in La Jolla on July 17, 2015, at age 74, from Multiple Myeloma. His beloved dog of 15 years, Sophie, followed him in death less than two weeks later.

Dr. Cassin received his Ph.D. in Molecular and Cellular Biology from Stanford University, followed by a postdoctoral fellowship in Marine Biology at Scripps Institution of Oceanography. He studied the molecular genetics of bioluminescence and chemiluminescence in marine bacteria, and the impact of agricultural wastewater on marine algal communities.

As the Executive Director of the Ocean Sciences Research Institute, Dr. Cassin was the Principal Investigator on an Office of Naval Research grant to study the molecular genetics of nitrate metabolism in marine phytoplankton. As a Visiting Scholar at Colombia's National Oceanographic Research Institution, the *Centro de Investigaciones Oceanográficas e Hidrográficas* in Cartagena, he managed a subsea mapping project off Colombia's Caribbean coast, advised the Colombian Navy on protection and conservation of historic shipwrecks in Colombian waters. He served as Chairman of the U.S. Department of Energy's (DOE) Technical Advisory Committee overseeing treatment and disposal of nuclear weapon wastes from 25,000 nuclear weapons decommissioned in compliance with SALT and START agreements with the former Soviet Union, and served as a member of DOE's Committee on Redirection of the National Laboratory System.

Over the years, Richard provided advisory services in coastal zone management, marine and aquatic ecosystems restoration, and policy development to public and private sector clients world-wide.

Richard is survived by Lynn, his wife of 23 years; step daughter, Tammy Reese, her son, Derek, and his son, Paul. To plant trees in memory, please visit the Sympathy Store[1]. Published by Ramona Sentinel on Aug. 7, 2015.

1.　　https://sympathy.legacy.com/en-us/funeral-flowers/

productdetails/?type=obituary&p=175458848&pn=richard-cassin&affiliateId=2756&sku=tre-tim&pm=240

Richard Wilkie

Opening to Another World:
Turning 19 at Mexico City College
Selections from my letters home and journals
April 9 to June 8, 1957 of my Freshman Year

PREFACE: The following writings during the last eight weeks of classes in my first year at Mexico City College illustrate how as a young American student at Mexico City College in the mid-to late-1950s I began to thrive in a multi-dimensional world of cultural diversity, stimulating and visual beauty of the landscapes, and in the Mexican people and in their way of life. I was in awe of the deep history and the range of opportunities for camaraderie and adventure that were there. The faculty and fellow students I found at Mexico City College between 1957 and January 1961 were very special and my experiences then have influenced my life ever since. It did not take long for me to realize that the orderly expectations of life back home in the States were dramatically altered once I entered Mexico.

MEXICO CITY—April 9, 1957 (Tuesday):

My birthday is in five days. I don't know whether I will feel 19 years old or not. Everyone here thinks that I am 22 or 23, but that is because most of them are that age or older—especially the military veterans on the G.I. Bill who are in their mid to late 20s and some even into their early 40s. Of the nearly 1000 or so students enrolled at MCC this academic year, about 400 are U.S. military veterans studying on the G.I. bill. Luckily, they get checks of $115 each month—what they referred to as "life blood." These older students—most of whom had fought in the Korean War, World War II, or both—add so much worldly experiences to every classroom discussion. In class the first day last fall I met Bob Dukes, an Air force veteran from Atlanta who had been a B-29 "tail-gunner" over Japan in WWII. His plane dropped the first supplies to an American POW camp on a mountainside only 12 miles from Nagasaki, where the second atomic bomb had exploded. Earlier in the mountains of Idaho in the late 1940s, my family heard stories about that same camp, and the first supplies that were dropped to it—from Tommy Burke, a friend of my parents who had been captured on Wake Island shortly after Pearl Harbor, and whose physical deterioration in that POW camp led to his early death in 1952.

For me, that link through time and space with Bob Dukes has been very meaningful. Not only am I learning to connect to places and events through personal experiences, but also—although once removed—I am connecting to historical events through people I know, and in this case from different perspectives of the same event. It is a powerful realization that connects me with people and history and the world. It is very different from just reading about events in books. Bob was about my age as a tail gunner in a B-29 over Japan in 1945—12 years ago. Because I am one the youngest students here at MCC, sometimes I feel 16, since my worldly life experiences have been relatively limited. I am listening and learning from their incredible life histories and adventures. If I had stayed in school in Idaho, I would have never had this opportunity to grow as a person, to travel and learn that there are many ways to look at life and to see the world. Every day here in Mexico I feel blessed!!!April 10, 1957 (Wednesday):

Last Saturday I really had two good games of softball in the tryouts for the Mexico City College (MCC) Azteca Softball Team. My team won both games. In the first game, I got two hits in three at bats, plus a walk. In the second game I walked four times—the only walks in the entire game, and I had all of them. I really had a great time playing. I have not made an error yet in the dozen or more games that we have played.

April 15, 1957 (Monday):

Well, I am now 19 years old! Yesterday on my birthday, Jim, a friend Don, and I climbed *Nevado de Toluca*—the fourth highest peak in Mexico at 15,390 feet. It is nearly 900 feet higher than the tallest mountain in the 48 lower United States—Mt. Whitney in California (14,495 ft.). It was beautiful! The only dangerous part was climbing several rock cliffs as it rained and snowed on us. Looking back after returning we realized that it was not a smart move to hike so late and with no lights or pickaxes because we would have been in major trouble if one of us had been injured. But we were glad we made the climb. It was amazing to look out to see blue sky above the stormy cloud line we were parallel with, and rain and snow below that. It was not your everyday perspective on the world.

We began the day at the Diana Fountain to meet for the Explorers' Club trip to *Nevado de Toluca,* but nobody with a car showed. The drivers had all signed up to go to the bullfights instead. It didn't look like any of the six of us who showed up were going anywhere until Don Koch said he had a car that was in bad shape but might make it, so four of us managed to get off on the trip by 8:30am. An earlier start would have been much better, but we had no choice.

The drive to *Nevado* took us west past Mexico City College at Kilometer 16 on the major two-lane highway to Toluca—where we stopped briefly to pick up sandwiches for our hike. The volcanic peak was only 40 kilometers south, but on a rugged dirt road where we soon blew out a tire. Luckily the spare tire was functional and we proceeded through the pine forests to an altitude above tree line at about 13,000 feet elevation. The country was magnificently rugged and the day a little stormy. The road was a bit like the Artillery Dome Road in Idaho's Wilderness Area: extremely narrow, a drop off of 4,000 feet or so on one side, and a spectacular view. At the lake we were at a high altitude alternatively opening and closing off blue sky.

We could not believe our eyes when a man, a woman, a young girl and a dog came walking across the floor of the crater where we parked the car at the trailhead. They were 20 miles from anywhere in the high mountains in an ice-cold wind. They had just come up the mountain from the south and were heading back up the road we came in on and when asked where they were going they waived up the road to the northwest. Before we all continued, we shared some of the food that we had just purchased in Toluca.

On the far side of the lake after 1pm, Jim, Don, Leroy and I took off to begin a 2000-foot climb over loose rocks climbing nearly straight up

Shortly after we started, we met three Mexican climbers that had finished their outing to the top of *Nevado de Toluca* while wearing warm clothes, carrying packs and supplies, using special loose rock-climbing shoes and carrying ice picks. They told us that we were "leaving too late in the day and you will never make it to the high crosses at the top, which are at an elevation of 4,576 meters" (15,016 feet).

Joking with them, we claimed we knew what we were doing, saying that "we had on our time-tested lower altitude hiking outfits of canvas sneakers perfect for snow, and we were wearing Levi pants and thin sweaters." Ha-Ha-Ha! ...But they did not laugh since we did not look like mountain climbers. As the Mexican climbers left us, we could hear them muttering "Stupid *gringos*."

At that point Leroy decided the Mexican climbers knew what they were talking about, so he turned back and told us he would "wait back at the car."

My Brother Jim wrote in a letter to our folks:

"The climb wasn't as hard as either Popocatepetl last fall or Dave Lewis Peak on the Middle Fork of the Salmon a few years ago at home, and we made it in 2 ½ hours while climbing mostly up into the clouds. We spent an hour on top and every now and then the clouds opened a bit and revealed the valley of Toluca and the sun streaking through the far sky in light rays coming through the storm."

Don Koch (left) and I are looking back down to the lake where we left our car.

We hated to go back down but we had fun sliding down the loose rockslides. The car was so cold we had a hard time getting out of the open-ended crater with the Lake, and the trip back was over a snow-covered road that included a splendid sunset to the West– a perfect day! Except that we had another flat tire back on the highway between Toluca and Mexico City. Lucky to be on a main highway instead of high on a freezing cold ridge, Jim and Leroy stayed with the car while Don and I hitched a ride into Toluca with one bad tire that had to be repaired. We didn't get home to Mexico City until long after midnight.

April 17, 1957 (Tuesday):

Everyday I continue to be impressed with the beauty of the MCC campus.

From the college there were magnificent views of the city to the east, the wooded *barranca* below the college, and on most days, the volcanoes *Popocatepetl* and *Iztaccihuatl* to the far south, which stood out against the horizon. The campus had taken over a former country club, so a number of buildings were already in place, including the two-story building housing the cafeteria, theater, and art department. The cafeteria opens on to a large open patio that projects out into the upper parts of old spreading eucalyptus trees from the slope below, with a lovely view south. On campus, the tiled mosaic murals on the walls of many of the open-air classrooms, along with the green, well-groomed campus with open patios and clusters of stone seating for outdoor seminars, gave the campus a strong aesthetic sense of belonging in its location. The campus fits with everything else around it along a beautiful wooded ridgeline rising to the west toward *Desierto de los Leones* [Desert of the Lions] National Park. Beyond is the pass to Toluca and its glorious Friday market. Everything about the place feels perfect!

Quetzalcoatl, Aztec God of Wisdom, sprawls on the lawn, regarding the modern activity of the
campus with age old eyes.

April 27, 1957 (Saturday):

Guess what? I was just hired to be in a Mexican movie. The name of the movie is "The Joaquin Capilla Story." He is the Mexican diver that won the only Mexican Gold Medal in the 1956 Olympics in Melbourne, Australia. [Actually, the name of the film ultimately was '*Paso a la Juventud*' – the Passing of Youth] Capilla is the star, along with TIN TAN (the famous Mexican comic) and the girl that represented Mexico in the Miss Universe contest. I play Gary Tobian, the American that came in second to Capilla by one-fifth of one point, to win the Silver Medal for the U.S. team in platform diving. I (playing Tobian) had beaten Capilla in the Pan American games the year before, so I am the main villain in the film. Luckily, I won't have to do any diving, since 'my stand-in' came in fifth in the Olympics. I will make about 170 Mexican pesos a day ($15 US) for up to five days of shooting. That $75 does not sound like much, but in Mexico where the per capita income for the year for the average person is only $178 (U.S.) a year, it is substantial. On May 7th they started filming my scenes.

Before I was hired, the Sub-Director and several others came out to Mexico City College and after watching students pass by between classes, asked me over to say the Director of a film wanted to meet me in the city after classes. When I did meet him, he offered me the role of Gary Tobian on the spot. He felt I looked a lot like Gary Tobian—we both had American styled crew cut hair—although Tobian was blond.

May 2, 1957 (Thursday):

Everything happened to me yesterday on May 1st —Mexico's Labor Day! I had a great time with friends on a picnic in the mountains with many of the softball players and their dates— including me with a blind date with a girl from Tennessee who is a model here in the city. We had a lot of fun playing softball, tossing footballs, and swimming in the crystal-clear springs—but I tore my knee out again playing the simple game of volleyball. I went up high to hit the volleyball but I came down and wrong and popped my knee. It is all swollen and I can't bend it. It really hurts, but it is not nearly as bad as my last injury with it in Boise in a football game. Now I probably will not be in the movie since I cannot walk properly. Damn it!

[Note: My football knee injury freed me from taking one of the University football scholarships I was offered back in the States, as it gave me the freedom to join my brother Jim at MCC. It is interesting that what I thought at the time was a heart-breaking unlucky event actually turned out to be one of the best things that ever happened to me. Looking back there is no way that football could ever have competed against the years of enjoyment I gained by going to Mexico City College.]

May 7, 1957 (Tuesday):

Today was the first day shooting the movie in which I am playing the role of Gary Tobian. I did not go to school, but went instead to the Olympic Pool at the University of Mexico at 8am. They had swimsuits and USA Olympic sweat suits for us, although at first the sizes were far too small. We ended up using regular swimsuits and they came up with larger USA sweat suits. We were not involved with the filming until 2 in the afternoon. All morning, we just watched the filming of the movie, and talked about the other stars in the movie. I had time to really get to know Bob Valentine—the American actor who played the third-place finisher. Before coming to MCC for a Master's degree he played guard on the University of Massachusetts football team. *[Note: Little could I have imagined that 10 ½ years later—in 1968—I would begin a 45-year career as a Professor at the University of Massachusetts.]*

I also enjoyed the time with the two Miss Mexico's in the film—Ana Bertha Lepe for 1955 and Erna Martha Bauman, for 1956. TIN-TAN—the Latin American comic version of Bob Hope-Danny Kaye—initially seemed distracted and then spent time amusing the others. The main star of the film—Joaquin Capilla—who won the only Mexican Gold Medal at the Melbourne Olympics last year—was the friendliest person on the set. Even he, however, got tired of waiting to shoot our diving scenes. I was surprised at how small he was in size, but that probably is an advantage when you are high diving from 32 feet 9 ¾ inches (10 meters) above the surface of the water. Thank heavens that my stand-in diver came in fifth in the Olympics. That height scared the hell out of me as I started to do handstands before they cut to a distance shot with my stand-in doing great dives. I am walking with quite a limp in the movie, but they did not seem to mind. The Director, G. Martinez Solares, and the movie's star Juaquin Capilla really treated Valentine and me as special.

Many people reminded us from time to time that the Olympic swimming pool is one of the most beautiful in the world, as if that was the only thing that was important—or—that they knew how to say it in English. We, of course, had enough Spanish by then to converse well enough in most situations, but many people wanted to practice speaking their English with us.

The Olympic Pool at the National University of Mexico, where the movie was filmed.

In the background to the southeast, are the peaks of Iztaccihuatl (17,454 ft. elevation) and Popocatepetl (17,887 ft.).

During the filming another male was used in the background that was supposed to be another American diver, but he looked like a cross between a gorilla and 'gorgeous George' the American wrestler. I guess they thought he would add to the 'gringo' stereotype of people from the United States, as well as the 'villains' that Valentine and I played.

[Note: I learned about villains the hard way when I saw the film in a Mexico City theater seven months later. The audience booed and jeered when I came on

the screen and some shouted 'Kill the Gringo!" I happened to look down into the seat on my left at the young man shouting to kill me. He turned and looked at me, then at the screen and saw me, then at me again as he fully realized the villain was sitting next to him. ...Then suddenly he exploded into total panic shouting—"Jesus Christo, Ayúdame!"— as he dove to try to squeeze under his seat. Luckily for me everyone else in the theater was concentrating and shouting at the Devil on the screen, and not the one in the seat chuckling to himself. But I also decided it was time to get out of that dark theater as quickly as possible before others recognized me. So, I fled out onto the Paseo de la Reforma and walked two blocks to our apartment.]

From the movie's poster: a photo of the three divers receiving their medals scene. I am on the left in 2nd place with USA on my uniform, Joaquin Capilla is

in the center in 1st place, and Bob Valentine is on the right in 3rd place, also with USA on his uniform.

May 11, 1957 (Saturday)

I played softball this morning. Even with my bad leg I was the first player chosen. In two games I had 3 hits in 7 times up and played shortstop. A Mexico City softball league has been formed with two teams from Mexico City College, the U.S. Embassy team—where sizable U.S. Marines contingency will also play for them—the Chapultepec Sports Club, Mexico City Sports Club, and several other teams. The Mexico City College—the '*Aztecas*' won the all-Mexico title last year and then went on to represent Mexico and to take third place in the World Championships held in Sacramento, California. A team from Florida took first place. The only loses for MCC were by scores of 2 to 1 and 3 to 2. I am excited about the prospects of making the team.

May 13, 1957 (Monday):

Wonderful News: I made first string on the Mexico City Softball team. It is the biggest team sport in the school and I really feel good about my selection. We really have a good team—and I mean GOOD. I really feel great that I made the starting team. My hitting has been about .400 (4 hits out of every 10 at bats) and I never make any errors. Out of about 600 men at school, 40 or so are good ball players. The 12 best players made the first team for the Mexico City league, and the next 12 made a second team for the league. Both MCC teams play separately.

The next youngest guy to me among the starters is age 21 and they go up to age 28 or so for two of them, since many are veterans and played on teams in the various services. Regarding the year in college of the top eleven players: four are seniors, four are juniors, two are sophomores, and I am the only freshman. Unfortunately, I will only get to play a quarter of the season as I have to return to Idaho to work for the summer. Joe Chase, the 1st baseman, is in the same boat as me, since every summer he has a fire-fighting job as a smokejumper in McCall, Idaho.

May 14, 1957 (Tuesday)

I had to miss school today because of the movie. To compound problems with my studies, tomorrow night we have a game under the lights. I have to do well if I want to keep my starting position.

Now I am hopelessly behind in all five courses. The movie is a wonderful opportunity but it is hurting me badly in the classroom. I was thinking of withdrawing from my classes, but I knew you [my parents] would both have a hemorrhage. Thanks for sending the *Idaho Daily Statesman* clipping about the Boise students at Mexico City College.

May 15, 1957 (Wednesday)

The transportation problem here in the city is getting worse every day. You can never catch a peso cab along the *Paseo de la Reforma* anymore, and the buses have people hanging out of them. The Government plans to build a subway, but it might be difficult as a city is slowly sinking. They are building a four-lane highway past the college, which means that they have been cutting down the big beautiful trees that are along the old highway in front of the college. What a loss, as the college entrance is now a lot of asphalt rather than the cool green beauty we had in the Spring and Winter Quarters. Some parking has been moved across the highway, but spaces are tight.

May 16, 1957 (Thursday):

God, what a difficult day yesterday! I was up at 7am and studied until 9am, ate breakfast, and went to school. I found Bill Valentine and told him they had notified us that we had to be back in the movie again to shoot the trophy award scenes. I went to my 11am class, but had to leave class early after ½ an hour so we could get to the movie set at the Olympic Pool all the way down near the National University. We were there being filmed receiving trophies for two hours. I came in second place with the Silver Medal, so I had to do some talking on the victory stand.

After the filming, Valentine and I tore home through the Mexico City traffic—a city in 1957 with a population of 4,734,000—to get home to change clothes and for me to get to the last pre-season exhibition ballgame where I started in Left Field. The first time I came to bat, we had runners on first and second bases, and nobody out. The coach gave me a sign to bunt and when I did, I beat it out to out to first to fill the bases. The next three batters popped up or struck out and I only got as far as second base, although one runner scored prior to that. The next time I came up with the bases loaded and walked. After the fourth inning we were ahead 5 to 4. The coach took out the entire first team so that the reserves could play, and we ended up losing the game 12 to 7. Our pitchers were not doing very well, but I am sure they will be ready for action in the league. I guess the coach needed to see how well all our players looked in game conditions. I arrived home at 9pm and just crawled into bed. What a day!

This morning, I was up early studying like mad for the final exams that are coming. We only have eleven more days of classes and then three days for testing.

May 20, 1957 (Sunday):

Recapping my dating experiences since returning to Mexico in January 1957:

The first girl that I went out with after I returned to Mexico City from Christmas break and my trip home and to the Rose Bowl was a Mexican girl, who had been the Mexico City College Queen for the main campus and the Mexican-English learning students. She was sweet and beautiful, but seemed quite serious about potential long-term commitments. I went out with her twice, but everything was quite expensive and I did not like the pressure to drop everything else I was doing, so I backed off. She asked me to her graduation dance in April, but I decided not to go. At least there are dozens of guys who would like to take her to the dance.

I went out twice with a girl from the University of Idaho who is attending classes at the University of Mexico at the south end of Mexico City. She started to really like me and also started talking about commitments, which was way too fast, so I backed off saying the bus commute to see her ate up huge chunks of time—which was true. While in Acapulco I went out on a casual date twice with a girl from the University of Oregon who was returning to Eugene after Winter Quarter a few weeks later. It is nice to just go out and have an enjoyable time away from studies and other obligations. It is always more fun to go to parties with a date, and my friend Murray usually has a date to accompany him. I went out one time to a party with a girl from Santa Ana, California, and once with Murray's girlfriend from Florida (before he started going with her). Finally, I also went to a party with a girl from a teacher's college in Connecticut.

Too bad my girlfriend in Boise and I agreed we should date and enjoy ourselves but not get serious. At that time, I had no idea these kinds of possibilities existed, but I feel I need to keep my commitments. I hope I am not being too naive. My friends say I am 'nuts!'

Sometimes parties could be hazardous. I also thought I had a date with a pretty Mexican girl that I met at a party at Freddie William's flat, but she gave me a time and place to meet her on the opposite side of Mexico City at a small restaurant. It took me two hours by bus at the worst time of day around 5 pm to get there. I waited and waited and finally asked the waiter if anyone knew her. No one had ever heard her name, but one of the waiters said several other 'gringos' had come there before but their date never arrived either. Clearly, she was leading them all on a wild goose chase. I heard later that apparently some Mexican women see it as a game, and they compete to see how many 'gringos' they can leave stranded in a distant location. All I could do was have a good laugh at myself and realize it was far easier to have a date with girls from MCC, especially since they were also pinching pennies and did not desire to spend a lot of money.

During the shooting of the movie, a Mexican movie starlet who is 17 or so, asked me when I am going to take her out? I was tempted, but my studies and upcoming final exams and summer absence—and my softball schedule with the MCC Azteca softball team—got in the way and I never had time to call her.

So, this time I will put the blame on my studies, since they have to come first and with 19 credits I am falling more and more behind every day. I also have the real excuse of not having the money to spend on expensive dates. My parents have sacrificed a lot already to send Jim and me to school all the way down here. At least I will make a few dollars in this film, which will help get Jim and I through until we leave. Technically foreign students are not supposed to earn money while on a 'tourist visa,' but everyone laughs at that rule. It is also odd that students come into Mexico on 'tourist visas' that are good for only six months, which means nearly all the students have to go to one border or another during the middle of the year to renew their visas, and of course that adds on to the expenses.

A number of our friends are virtually out of money at this point near the end of the term and are constantly asking each other for short-term loans. The lucky veterans only have to wait a few more weeks before they pick up their GI-bill payments.

I have never met so many really nice women in my life. Have I died and gone to heaven?

May 22, 1957 (Wednesday):

They finally found the body of the student that had been in my English class in the Fall Quarter. He had been robbed and killed outside of Acapulco.

[NOTE: I later wrote about that student's death in the memoir I authored entitled, "Dangerous Journeys: Mexico City College Students & the Mexican Landscape 1954-1972," which is online at the website: https://www.profmex.org/mexicoandtheworld/volume11/4fall06/mccchap__final.htm

"The final classmate to die —-from my English Writing seminar with only seven students—failed to return from a Thanksgiving week trip to Acapulco. He had gone to the famous bar, *Río Rita's*, in the red-light district with friends. Sometime around 2 am, when the student was totally drunk, he left to sleep in the back seat of their parked car outside the nightclub in a tough district of town. When his friends finally left *Río Rita's* a few hours later, the car was gone. The stranded students had to return to Mexico City the next day on a bus. It was about a half year later that the car was found about 50 miles from Acapulco on a side road over a cliff and burned to a shell, with the charred body of our classmate inside. The police said it was an accident, but his friends said it had to be murder. They never found his wallet or any of the things that were in the car.

During the last class in that course the four of us who were still alive after that short 10-week quarter looked at each other with relieved eyes—we had survived, while three had died!"16

That English Writing seminar with Brita Bowen certainly planted the seed for me to name the first part of my chapter 'Dangerous Journeys.' The other two deaths were from a drowning in Acapulco and a car wreck when a "Toluca Rocket" bus with bad brakes accidently beheaded the young driver (from Wyoming), as he backed out of the MCC parking lot in a low-cut sports car into traffic.

May 25, 1957 (Saturday):

Our League officially starts tomorrow. We play at 6pm and finish under the lights. I'm going to play as hard as possible. We had a practice game against the MCC second team (the Green Wave as we are the *Aztecas*). We won 8 to 2 after only four innings. I had one hit in two times at the plate, but I re-injured my knee again while sliding into third base.

May 26, 1957 (Sunday):

I have been sitting and adding up the mileage between Mexico City and Boise. It is 2,600 by the shortest route. Coming down here in Sept., via California, it was 3,450 miles. Going home at Christmas it was 2,970 to Boise, and 3,170 via stopping to see the Rose Bowl in Pasadena with Murray Pilkington and then traveling back to Mexico City to start the Winter Quarter. The roundtrip at Thanksgiving to Guatemala was 2,050 miles, and two trips to Acapulco and one to Veracruz during the year adds up to another 2,000 miles. By the time I return to Boise in June with another 3,000 miles, I will have traveled just over 19,000 miles in 9 months. If I had been traveling straight the entire time, I would have traveled three-fourths of the way around the world.

May 29, 1957 (Wednesday):

We won our game last Sunday 8 to 5, and I had one hit in two at bats. Unfortunately, I had to take time off from the team in order to pull my grades up for the final exams, and of course to let my knee recover. But since we will be leaving for Boise, I will miss only the game next Sunday. Most of the season will occur after I leave for Boise. It is hard for me that I just made the starting team and then must leave for the summer in Idaho to make enough money to be able to return to Mexico in September. At least I was told I'd automatically be on the team in the Fall Quarter when I return. My buddy John Freeman from Boise—who spent his freshman year at the University of Idaho—also wrote to say that he would be joining Jim and me next fall when we return to MCC. He was the baseball catcher at Boise High, so he should make the team.

June 1, 1957 (Saturday):

I am completely exhausted and tired from studying. After all this studying we will drive straight through in three days to Boise. I always do the night driving since I am the only one I can fully trust to not fall asleep at the wheel. At night, however, I can listen to the late-all night 10,000-Watt rock and roll music stations to keep me awake—one from Los Angeles and one from Chicago.

My studies are killing me! I was crazy to take an overload of 19 hours, when 15 hours is the normal load. I took my Anthropology Origins of Western Civilization final last Friday. God, it was hard and I could not fill in a number of the blanks. I will probably get a B in English Composition, Spanish Conversation, and Economics. As for Spanish Grammar (the hardest subject)—lord only knows! My two hardest tests are Monday—Spanish at 8am. Since last weekend all I have been doing is studying.

This drawing was in the MCC Collegian newspaper this week. I can relate to the dead guy as I feel like a zombie studying in the middle of the night.

Five of us—Murray Pilkington from California, Paul Dix—the rock climber from Spokane, Washington—Gil Heights from Brooklyn, Jim and I decided the pressure was too much, so we went out on a big drinking round to bid Mexico City College goodbye for the year. We got home at 3 am.

Today, I've studied all day and night. It is 12:15 am, and I have to get up at 7:30 to start studying again. Tomorrow is going to be the hardest day of studying that I have faced in my life. I do not relish the thought of getting up, but I know that when it is over, I will be on my way home.

Monday afternoon (June 3, 1957):

Good, my two hardest tests are over! Tomorrow my two easiest finals and then we will be on the road home. At the last minute, I am having very mixed feelings about leaving. Only one more night in this bed.

My grades sure have dropped. I think I will get three B's and two C's—maybe lower—but I had one hell of a great Spring Quarter. It's good that I had an A and four B's in Fall Quarter and two A's and two B's in the Winter Quarter. Because I did so well, I thought I could take 19 hours this time rather than 15, but that was a mistake.

[Note: Once grades came in, I did receive three B's—in Spanish grammar, Spanish Oral Speaking practice and English Composition—and two C's—in Origins of Western Civilization and Principles of Economics. I was really happy that I got a B in Spanish Grammar, my hardest course, but somehow my Economics course dropped to C. What happened there? Thus, for my full freshman year, I had three A's, nine B's and two C's—for a grade point average just above B. Not the best grades, but I was pleased because of my many other activities and adventures.]

Wednesday, early morning (June 5, 1957):

After classes we packed late on Tuesday night and the five of us hit the road at dawn straight north via San Luis Potosi, Saltillo, Monclova and finally out of Mexico at Piedras Negras into Eagle Pass, Texas at the U.S. border and then north.

Driving Home to Boise from Mexico City: June 5-8, 1957

The drive home to the States was quite meaningful for me, as the drives back and forth to Mexico were an extremely important part of the greater Mexico City College experience. Driving in the middle of the night gave me time to ponder what I had learned throughout the year and place everything into perspective. Isn't that why I came down to Mexico in the first place—to study and learn? But I was having such a good time throughout the year I had little time process it all and reconsider my life.

We left Mexico City on June 5, 1957, driving home with Joe Chase--our first baseman—back to Idaho. We reached Boise three days later on June 8th after a marathon drive. Joe headed to his smoke-jumping job in McCall, brother Jim to his surveying job for the Bureau of Public Roads also in McCall and me to a dangerous job as tail-sawyer in a lumber saw mill near Boise, and later I became a member of the firefighting crew for the Bureau of Land Management. Mike Johnson did not have a job yet, so he rode with us as far as Salt Lake City and then spent the summer in the San Francisco area.

I did the night driving since I trusted no one else for the job after Bill Shear fell asleep at the wheel during a night drive on our trip down to Mexico last September. Luckily my brother Jim was sitting next to Bill and woke up just in time to grab the steering wheel seconds before we peeled off into a canyon at about 50 miles per hour. That was just the first of our many close calls in Mexico over the next three years.

For our trip north during my night driving shifts I took one *Benzedrine* pill every three or four hours to keep me awake during the wee hours of the night. I wanted to remain super alert to everything I was seeing and doing, as well as thinking about what I had learned during my year at MCC. Students in Mexico used these pills to study all night for tests—even though I did not. MCC veterans said *Benzedrine* and *Dexedrine* pills were standard in military operations, especially among airplane pilots. But taking *Benzedrine* to stay awake and arrive home alive was a cheap insurance policy worth taking.

The most memorable part of our more than 3,000-mile drive back to Idaho that year was the second night while driving through empty west Texas. I was roaring through the night under a full moon with no other cars on the road—feeling a bit high while totally alert—as I sped along at 80 to 90 miles per hour. The road was the straightest and emptiest of other vehicles that I had ever experienced. It also turned out to be one of the craziest—most surrealistic—nights I can remember. I could not believe my good fortune and I felt like an astronaut hurtling through space.

Late Night Radio:

In this part of west Texas most of the AM stations carried crazy country right-wing preachers and cowboy "she dun left me" songs. I had never been exposed before to the insane screaming of preachers railing at communists, non-Christians, and the U.S. government, but their ranting certainly captured a sense I was on an alien planet. I had been raised in what I describe as a "mountain culture" where everyone was positive and wanting to help each other in troubled times. Democrats, Republicans, whatever, it did not matter.

The people I knew were not always trying to blame others for problems they were experiencing. In the mountains there was more of a Scandinavian cultural outlook, or of mining or lumbering town cultures that seemed to give a message that "we are here for each other." People looked inward and not outward for answers to their lives. They normally thought for themselves rather than being told what and how to think and who to blame. Somehow the "cowboy culture" of the lone self-made man did not permeate up into mountainous central Idaho. I admired cowboys, but they were often loners and all too often negative. All the plains and ranching country farther south seemed to be "cowboy country." At least that was my experience in the mountains of central Idaho as I grew up in the late 1940s and early 1950s.

The message that poured through the night airwaves was at times deafeningly negative, fearful, and terribly depressing if I had bought into it—but I didn't—as it represented the antithesis of the kind of person I wanted to be, and to the kind of people I wanted to share my life with as friends and community. It was something not found in Mexico where people at all levels seemed friendly and positive most of the time.

In early June 1957 the U.S. still had 10,000-watt long-distance AM radio stations that had a reach of several thousand miles. Over the three days on this drive—especially as we got farther west—I really liked the disk jockey "Wolfman Jack" out of Modesto, California with the California sounds. Farther east in Texas the best I could do that night was a more liberal all-night talk show out of Chicago that occasionally wafted in through the static airwaves.

Beyond anything I had listened to before were the crazy "wild-screaming" preachers out of the Bible belt states. They ranted and raved by the hour over every right-wing idea that ever existed and they begged and cajoled their audiences to solve everything by sending them money as quickly as possible. All I could imagine were poor little dirt farmers scraping together their hard-earned money to send to those vultures. I could only wonder what rock those crazies crawled out from under? For them, everything is a "world conspiracy" against God and the Christian World...and the Republican Party!

Thus, the airwaves in the U.S. provided a sharp contrast with the mostly Mexican songs being played in Northern Mexico. My favorite regional music in Mexico was the Huapango style from Veracruz and Gulf of Mexico region that we had experienced live in Veracruz last November. Some of our favorites had been '*Malagueña Salerosa*' and '*La Bamba*'—Veracruz style that included harps.

So here I was returning to Boise where it previously was nearly impossible to talk with some members of the John Birch Society about politics or anything logical, but these crazy night-radio preachers appeared to be even more extreme. Their fervor and rants to send them money kept me amused for a time as I ripped down the west-Texas highway, although I kept scanning the dial for relief. Ads for sudden medical cures or a special balm for hemorrhoids kept popping up on the dial, but finally as we drove farther west the music stations from California started to come in on the dial more strongly as all options from Mexican music stations faded out. Fortunately, my singing along with the Eberly Brothers on 'Wake Up Little Suzy and Bye-Bye Love', 'That'll Be the Day' with Buddy Holly and the Crickets, Elvis's 'All Shook Up' and many other songs, did not seem to bother my car load of sleepers as we seemed to be gliding down the highway on a magic carpet.

A Sudden Series of Events

What did bother them, however, was that all of sudden a skunk was crossing the road and there was no way to miss him at the speed I was going. My headlights saw him coming at the last minute, but too late. The slightest swing of the wheel to avoid him at 85 miles an hour could have been disastrous, so I smacked him going full speed. The thump sound surprised me, but what really blew me away was the 'horrific stench' that quickly permeated the inside of the car. As the sleepers woke up grumbling about "What the hell is that god-awful stench?" type comments, all I could say was, "I think that big skunk flipped up into the undercarriage of the car and is still traveling with us." Everybody started laughing, and we continued roaring down the highway as the smell failed to recede and our noses became numb.

As everyone was roaring with laughter, the next thing I knew the car left the ground as the roadway took a sudden dip down into an *arroyo* and small stream crossing. I had not seen the dip in advance because of our speed and when the tires came back onto the road. Whoopees... and strangled laughs accelerated from my companions. Then, out of nowhere, a giant armadillo was crossing the road, and I hit it square on. BOOM! What a surprise: it was like hitting a 90-pound giant raw egg, as its interior exploded almost in liquid form. While I struggled to keep control of the car, we shot up the opposite side of the *arroyo* where we left the ground again. Coming back down on the road at such speed was a bit scary, but my experience driving our pickup truck at our mountain lodge in Idaho had me prepared for these kinds of surprises.

This added to the laughter of our group of intrepid gringos, when suddenly about 5 miles farther down the highway, a large object loomed into the headlights as I bore down on it at break-neck speed. When I thought I would hit the dark object hunched in the middle of the road, it suddenly leapt into the air and threw out a black wingspan that virtually covered the entire windshield before it disappeared into the night directly above the top of our car. In a flash my breath was totally taken from me as if I were gut punched—and I ducked—thinking the monster or whatever it was would come crashing through the windshield.

Clearly a large black bird—perhaps a Turkey Vulture—had been eating a dead animal in the road, and as it covered the windshield with its wingspan it scared the "beJesus" out of me at high speed. I recovered fast, however, and those who were awake roared with laughter once again. Knowing I could not take any more of these surprises I decided to reduce speed slightly to around 75 miles per hour. And still, we were the only vehicle on the highway

After a time, the others were asleep again following the incident with the bird, but most of what I had to listen to was going back to the crazy preachers on the radio starting in again attacking the "International Monetary Fund" and the evil world control of our country by Communists and "Commie-Liberals." I even tried to follow their logic for a time, but it was impossible to find anything constructive from their ranting. I just could not understand how the idea that 'Liberals'—who believe in an open pluralist society for all citizens, with access to education, jobs, health services, voting rights, housing and free travel that are open to everyone, and free flows of information, ideas and a free press cannot be limited by government or authoritarian powers—could be associated in the minds of right-wingers as being the same thing as what Communists want for their societies. So, I decided their ranting had nothing to do with reality.

Communist regimes want Totalitarian control from the top-down of everyone in the name of the state, but of course the state is merely the tyrannical Ruler or Dictator who is the law and who controls how their subjects can think and what they are allowed to discuss. Liberals—and Democratic socialist countries like the ones in Scandinavia—could not be any farther away ideologically from the Totalitarian extreme left—or from the extreme Authoritarian right wing—for that matter— as they too seem to want 'Dictators' who will destroy democratic principles and governments. The extreme right also desires to control the minds and bodies of their followers: "Keep them dumb and uneducated and they will believe anything!"

So, the night went on as I pondered the things I was hearing on the radio on the

American side of the border compared to what I had been hearing and experiences south of the border. Mexico seemed to me to be a softer, friendlier culture dominated by a nurturing "Mother Mexico" image while the harshness, anger, almost hate that came from the sterner "Uncle Sam" to the north seemed not so friendly. I realized then how much the soul of Mexico had seeped into my views of life, which also echoed how life had been in the Salmon River country of Idaho in the way that people thought and cared about one another.

In Mexico, I remembered countless scenes of families and people enjoying life together, even under difficult times economically. Yes, Mexico had gone through a major Revolution for social change and land reform between 1910-1925, but life for most people was far superior to what they had previously under President (for Life) Porfirio Diaz between 1877 and 1911, when large Haciendas held almost all the land and the countryside was ruled by their often cruel "*Rurales*" policemen who could shoot or hang almost anyone they felt was making trouble.

The spirit of the Mexican Revolution lived on during the time Mexico City College existed, and although people continued to struggle for a better life, they now had much more than they had prior to the Revolution. I could see it and feel it in the smiles of people, who often went out of their way to be friendly—not only to us but to each other. "*Viva la Revolucion!*" was a term I often heard or saw signs that reminded people of what the vast majority of Mexicans saw as a major step forward.

It was then too that I vowed to look for the best in peoples and their cultures, and it made me want to explore the world even more. I developed a strong desire to document the everyday life of people visually and with words, and it is something I have spent the rest of my life doing.

In the middle of the night in the middle of a vast empty landscape I stopped the car so everyone could get out and relieve their bladders. After getting back underway, I returned to my private world of searching for music on the night radio, fight off the sounds of 'crazy preachers' and watching the clouds slip back and forth in front of the full moon over the west Texas landscape.

I was already daydreaming—excuse me: night dreaming—about returning to Mexico in the September for my sophomore year at Mexico City College.

So yes: it was a surrealistic night I will never forget!

What I Learned from my First Year at MCC:

Why did I focus on writing about the last eight weeks near the end of my freshmen year at Mexico City College—just as I turned 19 years of age?

Writing this memoir gave me the opportunity to relive a crucial "turning point" that ultimately led to a scholarly life in academia.

While I was struggling to mesh my studies with my activities, I was also making a major intellectual decision about my future life. It was rewarding and exciting to have that breakthrough, and it most likely only happened because MCC pushed students to engage not only with their courses and the college, but to explore and interact with all dimensions of the Mexican milieu—the people, their history and culture, their language with 62 distinct languages in 100 dialects, their Mexican diet that uses crops that were first in the world to be develop such as tomatoes, corn, squash, scallions and their various regional styles of music and dance. Living in a broad range of ecologies and geographies people seem to have a special understanding of the importance of places in their lives.

As I turned 19 while at MCC, I was already reaping the benefits from my initial time there. I had no idea that eight years after my freshman year at MCC, I would become a "Fulbright Scholar" to Argentina (Sept. 1965 to March 1967), or that eleven years later in January 1968, I would begin an academic life as a professor of geography and geosciences at the University of Massachusetts, Amherst. My career at UMass lasted 44½ years to 2012. I kept my office there for five more years and my last Ph.D. student finished in 2018—50 years after I first arrived at UMass.

My M.A. and Ph.D. at the University of Washington—Seattle were a necessity for my career, but I give much of the credit for my early moves forward to my brother Jim and the faculty and fellow students at MCC for inspiring me to think about becoming an academic. Thus, I had many mentors at MCC involved in the early stages of that process.

MCC was unique as a center for higher education in Latin America with the kinds of breadth and depth in quality education and courses that were readily accepted at colleges and universities in the U.S., Canada and Europe. In addition, I feel that ex-Mexico City College students and graduates often got a step up for their academic positions involving Latin America because they had hands-on-experiences in Mexico that many others did not have.

It is important to note that it was not only me that found studying at Mexico City College an important step in shaping a future academic career. When I first came to the University of Massachusetts in 1968, I discovered that six other ex-MCC students also were on the faculty in the joint Five Colleges Association: the University of Massachusetts, Amherst College, Smith College, Mount Holyoke College and Hampshire College. At the time the consortium had one of the strongest Latin American Studies Programs in the country.

Considering the small size of Mexico City College, having six faculty with time and/or degrees from MCC in western Massachusetts seemed like an extraordinary number. Clearly it showed the outreach and impact that MCC had on many institutions of higher education in the United States and elsewhere.

The Miguel Covarrubias (MCC Professor) mural honoring Mexican indigenous cultures and landscapes. Created in 1947 in the Hotel Del Prado's lobby in Mexico City, the 1985 Earthquake destroyed it.

The Arrival, c. 1957

A Fable

Charles was early.

With no passengers in it, the terminal appeared abandoned. The only other person present, an elderly worker, swept aimlessly in a far corner. It was hot and sunny outside and gloomy inside, or at least that was how Charles experienced it. His self-esteem shattered, everything looked dismal to him.

The expansive waiting room had a low ceiling and a few large windows. Stained and dirty, its floor reminded Charles of his childhood movie theater, with its decades of sticky debris stomped into the carpeting. Named the "Rialto," everyone called it "The Itch."

"Well, it's not that bad," Charles thought. "At least it doesn't have a stale cigarette stench."

Instead of chairs, there were broad backless wooden benches. Charles sat down on one of them, put his suitcase at his feet, and surveyed the room. At the other end was a check-in counter with no staff present.

He had not thought much in advance about the Tijuana Airport. Having partied in the town several times, he had few positive expectations. TJ had a reputation as an expansive series of brothels and sex shows, with sidewalks crammed with glittery souvenirs and donkeys for tourist photos.

However, the waiting area's condition caused him to worry about the plane.

"If it's anything like the terminal," he thought. "I'm not getting on it."

Charles' only luggage, the suitcase, contained a change of clothes, a jacket, a pair of shoes, the preliminary divorce papers, a power of attorney, the address and phone number of a Mexico City lawyer, and a book to read. His driver's license, birth certificate, the tourist card he got at the border, plane tickets, and thirty dollars were in his pockets. In retrospect, he wondered what he thought he was doing, having only thirty dollars and not speaking more than a few Spanish phrases. Worse yet, no one would greet him at the capital's airport; he did not know anyone in Mexico City.

His parents drove him to the LA Greyhound station. If they were concerned about his trip, they did not say so. He thought just as well, not wanting to hear any useless warnings. He figured they were also in shock because of recent events.

Soon on a San Diego bus, he boarded another to the border, got his tourist card, and took a shuttle to the nearby airport. It was a smooth trip, but he hardly noticed it. Flying into the unknown had not worried him; deep in denial, he was about as out of touch with immediate reality as one could be and still function. He imagined Mexico City as a large Tijuana and not that much of a challenge. Later, more than ashamed and embarrassed about having such a ridiculous image of Mexico's capital, he was glad he never mentioned it to anyone.

However, the condition of the terminal got past the mental wall he was using to cope. Never having flown before, his doubts continued to surface, and he began to feel uncomfortably anxious. Just then, passengers arrived; well dressed and friendly, they said hello or nodded. Most of them appeared to be upper-class Mexicans; an American woman wearing a casual business suit was among them.

"If these are the passengers, the plane cannot be that bad," he thought, relaxed, and went back to reading Somerset Maugham's *Of Human Bondage* to pass the time. He was painfully aware of the irony of this book's themes, given the events precipitating his trip.

"Looks like someone was smart enough to bring along reading material," the American woman chuckled.

Charles almost flinched.

"She is striking up a conversation with me?" his mind sputtered. Attractive, probably in her mid-30s, and well dressed, he felt intimidated by her.

He smiled, not saying anything, wondering why she would talk to an overweight 18-year-old in great despair.

"My name is Maisie," she said and sat beside him. He introduced himself, and they chatted until their flight was announced.

She said she was from San Francisco.

* * *

Three weeks earlier, he and his friends, Jim and Malcolm, left Willits in Northern California before dawn. They planned to reach Pasadena by evening, over 700 miles to the south. An unplanned detour to Lake Tahoe, where they had lunch and gambled, slowed them considerably. It was about 10pm when they reached Mojave, having traveled down the eastern side of the Sierra Nevadas. Two more hours to go, and Charles had done all the driving. It was his car, a hopped-up '49 Chevy sedan. In a semi-trance and grossly fatigued, it never crossed his mind to ask one of them to take over. The promise of a hot shower and a comfortable bed kept him going.

The closer they neared Pasadena, the more his friends—who never offered to get in the driver's seat—kidded him. They would have to sleep on cold, empty mattresses while he enjoyed connubial bliss with his wife. Ha, ha. Keeping his concentration on the road because he had started nodding off, he laughed with them, even though he did not appreciate their jibes and was worried about his arrival.

His marriage was more than troubled. The four-day trip was supposed to be a time-out to think about their next move. Since they married two years earlier, he had graduated from high school and completed his first year in college while working full time. Would he go into the Army? Would they go somewhere to have a fresh start? He had not mentioned his concerns to his friends or sought their advice. For the most part, he avoided thinking about it. He felt trapped and could not imagine a solution to his dilemma.

They wound their way from Lancaster over the San Gabriel Mountains to Pasadena. He dropped his friends off and drove home. The house was empty. His wife and their one-year-old daughter were not there.

"Perhaps they are with her parents," he thought. Too tired to call, he took a shower and headed for bed.

A few steps from lying down, he noticed a sock up against the bedroom baseboard. He realized it had been in the same spot four days earlier. A sense of dread erupted in his lower abdomen. Without thinking about it, he searched in their dresser. A checkbook and two savings account books were in the top drawer. All three were empty, canceled out.

* * *

A few months before his trip, Charles caught his wife, Tam, in an affair with her boss, Eric.

One night after dinner, she told Charles about attending an Avon sales meeting. However, both their cars required minor repairs, which he planned to do the next day. Tam said she asked a fellow "Avon Lady" to give her a ride, and she had requested Tam to wait at the corner. It was already dark outside, so Charles offered to carry her sample case and stay with her.

"No, no, that's not necessary," she said nervously, making him suspicious. He also wondered why her friend was not coming to the house to pick her up.

Standing under the streetlight's circle of light, Tam kept fidgeting. Charles was about to ask her about it when a car appeared out of the dark. Even before seeing his face, Charles recognized her boss's Hudson. As he got closer, Tam waved him on. He sped by, hunched down behind the steering wheel.

Charles felt like a baseball bat had slammed into his lower abdomen. Stunned speechless, a whole series of past incidents, situations, and his wife's frequent comments about how "cool" her boss was, came into focus; this had been going on for some time.

Predictably, Tam denied everything. Eric was just giving her a ride. Charles did not bother to point out that if it were true, why did she signal him to keep going, and why had he accelerated past them, his head low? Her version was ridiculous; besides, he was no Avon Lady.

Furious, Charles borrowed a neighbor's car and drove to Eric's home to confront him. When he arrived, he realized Eric was alone; his wife and kids were away.

They sat facing each other, Eric ludicrously denying everything. Charles held a nine-shot, .22 caliber revolver in his jacket pocket, pointed at the boss's groin, ready to pull the trigger.

Eric was a 35-year-old successful Swiss businessman with a "trophy wife," two children, and an Altadena home with a large swimming pool. Charles felt painfully inadequate compared to him and enraged that he had taken advantage of his teenage wife. However, he was sure Tam had delighted in Eric's advances, having spoken about wanting to have sex with others. Eric's grinning, deceitful manner made Charles even angrier. His finger tightened on the trigger as he imagined pressing it repeatedly until the revolver was empty.

At that moment, a voice shouted inside his head, "Do not throw away your life. Things change."

Charles realized that if he shot Eric, he would face a dismal future and took his finger off the trigger. He valued his life more than exacting revenge.

* * *

After the shocking return to the empty house, Charles learned the next day that his wife had moved in with a co-worker, recently released from San Quentin. He was into drag racing and knew about her relationship with their boss. She had emptied their bank accounts to rent an apartment for them.

Rejection is an "ego-smasher," but it also meant freedom to Charles.

The quality of their marriage had become increasingly toxic after he discovered her betrayal. Depressed, his sleep and appetite disturbed, he lost all the motivation that had kept him in school while working at $1.25 to $2 an hour jobs. Sleep deprivation and general fatigue added to his growing unhappiness. Partially in denial, he passive-aggressively punished his wife, no doubt pushing her toward her decision. He felt stuck in the marriage with no acceptable exit. His parents, his infant daughter, a Catholic upbringing, and not wanting to be the "bad guy" made getting a divorce out of the question. Nevertheless, he continued to suffer considerable emotional pain.

After the hurtful discovery, he decided to take a semester off from college and explore their life options in detail. The brief trip was part of that process. He came back, however, without a clue about their future. His wife, however, solved his quandary.

Dumped, he moved back home, which simultaneously felt like a defeat and a rescue from a burning building.

A week later, his wife called and asked him to meet with her and her lawyer the next day.

What transpired during that meeting was life-changing for Charles, although he did not realize its full scope for several years.

The sugary-talking lawyer-—who seemed more like a used car salesman to Charles—-explained that he could only represent one party. Because of that, he offered only to facilitate communication between them. Charles immediately stated that he would do whatever was necessary for the divorce. His demeanor surprised his wife and her lawyer; perhaps they expected him to make it as difficult as possible. Tam asked him if he would get the divorce because it would take a year in California but accomplished quickly in Las Vegas or Mexico City. She added that "they" would pay all the expenses.

Again, he agreed without hesitation.

Charles thought, "I've been to Las Vegas several times; I might as well go to Mexico City."

It did not cross his mind that he did not know how to get there, did not speak Spanish, did not know anyone there, did not have any money, and did not know what challenges staying for several weeks might present.

Cynically, it pleased him that she and her ex-con paramour, George, would pay for his "Mexico City vacation." He figured they would be highly motivated to get the divorce. Moving in with somebody else's wife probably would not look good to George's parole officer. The sooner they could marry, the better.

The lawyer gave Charles the name, address, and phone number of a Mexico City colleague. Tam came up with a hundred dollars to start the trip and committed to wiring him more money while he was in Mexico. Given how much they wanted the divorce, he did not consider the possibility of becoming marooned without funds.

Uncomfortable in her presence, Charles did his best not to show it. He knew she seemed incapable of experiencing guilt; that or she thought his behavior after Eric's "drive-by" justified hers. Charles was the bad guy. He felt hurt and relieved every time he thought about what had happened. Secretly, he thanked her for releasing him from his "prison." He did not forgive her, though, for the betrayal and rejection.

Avoidance became a favored coping mechanism; he spent little time in touch with his feelings. Traveling to Mexico seemed perfect to him.

* * *

Stepping outside the terminal, a marvelous sight greeted Charles. The passengers ahead of him were climbing into a gleaming Lockheed Constellation. Planes had fascinated him since childhood, and he knew the "Connie" was a highly regarded airliner. Sleek, with four motors, a shining aluminum fuselage, and a tripletail, it looked like it was flying while parked on the tarmac.

Charles felt better.

Not having paid much attention to the airport's location, he could see now that the border fence was not far from the end of the runway. It seemed strange to have takeoffs and landings so close to an international border, especially with a runway perpendicular to it.

Once inside the plane, he found his window seat and settled in. Flight attendants gave smiling welcomes and guided the other passengers down the aisle. The loading of passengers, luggage, and fueling completed, the engines started, one by one, coughing and then roaring.

Taxiing to the end of the runway, the Constellation turned around and accelerated toward the US. It took off and quickly climbed above the airport. Charles gazed at the town and desert-like landscape while enjoying the thrill of his first plane ride. Unexpectedly, the pilot began an abrupt 180-degree turn. Charles looked down the left wing pointed toward the ground and watched a tiny pickup truck making its way along a dusty road. He felt a surge of fear, imagining the airliner falling sideways out of the sky. There was a flurry of activity in the cabin, but Charles paid little heed. Enthralled with his first flight, he now felt terrified. The smell of vomit explained the earlier sounds; passengers had grabbed puke bags out of the seatback pockets. He started to laugh but suppressed it.

He imagined the border was a factor in the wrenching, nausea-precipitating U-turn. Years and many flights later, Charles never again experienced anything like that takeoff. In retrospect, he wondered if it was an omen.

* * *

Dozing, Charles awakened to the announcement of their Mexico City arrival, just past midnight. He gazed out the window and felt a wave of anxiety; there were lights as far as he could see. It was a big city, which he had not envisioned. As it descended, the plane seemed to be headed for the capital's outskirts.

"Where am I staying tonight?" he asked himself without having an answer.

"Why didn't I do some research about the city? I don't even have a guidebook with me!" he chided himself, reality painfully coming into focus.

He had the lawyer's address and phone number, which could be his starting point. Perhaps he could have the divorce started in a few days, sign some papers, and fly home. The Pasadena lawyer made it sound like ordering a hamburger at a drive-in restaurant. Charles relaxed.

" I can do this," he told himself.

The Constellation landed smoothly. He almost laughed at his previous worries about what kind of a plane and pilots would fly out of Tijuana. The trip felt luxurious, with two meals, plenty of (alcoholic) drinks, and no fighter plane aerobatics.

While the other passengers were milling around and greeted by friends or relatives, he picked up his suitcase at the baggage counter and walked outside the central doorway. It was near one o'clock in the morning, and blackness extended in all directions. There was one desultory streetlight and a few cabs along the sidewalk.

"The airport must be far from the city," he imagined.

At that moment, panic erupted.

"Where am I going to stay? What have I gotten myself into? Christ, I can't even speak Spanish!"

His panic increased as a threatening reality crashed through his wall of denial and avoidance.

"This is ridiculous! OK, I have a roundtrip ticket. I can fly back to Tijuana."

He turned around and walked briskly back into the terminal. Heading for the ticket counter, he wondered when the next flight would take off.

Maisie, the woman from San Francisco, stopped him. They had enjoyed a pleasant conversation during the flight, the free drinks helping him feel somewhat confident. She was on a package vacation in the city: airfare, hotel, meals, rides to and from the airport, and tickets to several attractions. Her guide stood to one side, waiting to take her to the hotel.

"I've got meal vouchers, so why don't we have lunch tomorrow? You will only have to pay for yours," she suggested with a smile.

Charles did not immediately reply.

She wants to have lunch with me? He thought in disbelief. Finally, he stuttered, "Sure."

"Great. I'm staying at the Hotel Bamer. Here's the telephone number; call me tomorrow," she added with another smile. Then, she walked towards the exit with her guide.

Befuddled, Charles juggled her unexpected invitation with his urge to get on the next plane headed for the border.

He took a few more steps towards the counter when Rodrigo, a Peruvian he had talked with during the flight, touched him on the shoulder and exclaimed with a laugh, "Well, you beat me to her; good for you!"

Charles was close to cognitive lockdown and only began to open his mouth when Rodrigo asked, speaking rapidly, "Hey, got a hotel booked in town? If not, we could look for one together. I don't want to spend a lot. There are some good ones at very reasonable rates if you avoid the tourist traps."

Still attempting to catch up with what was happening, Charles replied, "Sure."

"*Que Bueno!* I have several big game rifles with me, and I need to store them securely here at the airport. I plan to stay a few days before continuing to Lima. Do you mind tagging along? It shouldn't take a great deal of time."

Charles nodded his agreement, and they walked to the counter. Rodrigo began speaking Spanish so fast that Charles understood almost none of it. He wondered if any of his high school Spanish would return. Rodrigo was smooth-talking a uniformed airport man and a woman in a business suit, who Charles guessed worked for the government. The discussion lasted a few more minutes, and then the man gestured for Rodrigo to come behind the counter.

Over his shoulder, Rodrigo quickly told Charles, "We've got to go to a government office to get clearance. OK?"

Charles nodded, and they walked out a door that opened to an area of offices in the terminal's back wall. The government woman stayed behind. Facing them was a line of planes parked for future flights or repairs. They got into a large utility van parked just outside the door. There were no seats in the back, so he and Rodrigo sat cross-legged on the metal floor, and the driver and the official sat in front. Going only a short distance along the outside wall, Rodrigo produced a bottle of Tequila from his travel bag that quickly made the rounds. With the first slug, Charles began to feel much better.

They stopped in front of a small office with a counter facing the airstrip. Getting out of the van, Charles noticed a DC-3, an iconic aircraft from the Second World War, in a hanger farther down the line. He wanted to look it over but did not say anything. It seemed strange to be in an area only for authorized personnel.

He paused to gaze at the DC-3 while Rodrigo and the airport official entered the office ahead of him. When he got inside, the Tequila bottle was again making its rounds. Rodrigo was doing his best to arrange for his guns—a la shots of Tequila—without paying large bribes.

Only knowing the context, Charles kept his mouth shut and did nothing to interfere with Rodrigo's banter. The Tequila kept flowing; everyone laughed at jokes Charles could not understand but started laughing anyway. It had been five hours since his last meal on the plane, and he was becoming quickly inebriated, as were the other men. He was surprised when everyone, including the man in the office, got into the van. They drove farther down the line to another office, where there were several men, two of them in shiny business suits. The tequila bottle rapidly evaporated as it made its rounds without a pause.

Charles stopped paying attention to what was happening, stepped outside the office, and stared at the DC-3, now closer. It was a WWII mainstay for cargo, troops, and even the D-day paratroopers. Not as sleek as the Connie, it did have swept-back wings and a sturdy aluminum fuselage.

A fresh bottle of Tequila appeared inside the office, perhaps from the officials. A few more swigs and everyone got into the van and drove to another office. When they got there, Charles stayed in the vehicle. For the moment, he did not want more Tequila.

Almost falling asleep while Rodrigo did his convivial best to influence the officials, he was startled when everyone noisily returned to the van. With the guns securely stored, Rodrigo was happy and laughing, as were the other men. Tequila continued to flow.

Charles blurted loudly after taking another swig, "Where's my suitcase?"

Thoroughly intoxicated, there was a high-pitched note of anxiety in his voice. He had nothing with him, having placed his ID, tourist card, money, and return plane ticket in the suitcase for safekeeping when they exited the terminal.

A search began in the darkness, and they backtracked from one office to another. The suitcase had disappeared.

Charles wondered if someone had stolen it while everyone was in one of the offices. He did not say anything, frozen in panic.

At the last office, the men asked if he had taken the suitcase out of the van. No, he had not. The search would continue. He felt close to fainting.

Still frantic, Charles discovered he was sitting on his suitcase.

* * *

The suitcase crisis took some of the edge off Charles' Tequila high, but he was still inebriated when they walked out of the terminal. In his late 20s or early 30s and well built, Rodrigo never seemed to stop talking. On the plane, he told Charles he had just graduated from Cal Poly and was going home to take over his family's hacienda. Charles did not know whether to believe Rodrigo's self-important tales but decided not to question them. Rod was a life preserver thrown to him as he sank into an adrenaline-poached frenzy, ready to turn tail and fly back to familiar Southern California.

There was only one taxi at the curb, the driver leaning against it. No more planes were coming in until morning, and later Charles wondered why the cabbie was there because the terminal was empty. They jumped into the cab, and Rodrigo began his Spanish rap with the driver, who seemed so friendly that Charles worried he might take them for a "ride." Rodrigo, who appeared quite wise in the Latin ways of doing things, was happily conversing with him, which calmed Charles. Rod passed the driver a bottle of Tequila, and it began to make its rounds again.

(To his painful shame, Charles never learned the name of the *taxista*. Years later, reading Carlos Castaneda, he wondered if he was an ally to guide him through his first hours in the Mexican capital. He was no ordinary taxi driver.)

Charles caught a few phrases now and then as Rodrigo and the Taxista discussed finding a suitable hotel. Reaching the city, they drove past the Zocalo, the central square. After another twelve or more blocks, they stopped in front of the Hotel San Cosme.

What happened at that point is still a mystery to Charles. The driver parked the car and went inside the hotel with them. The concierge, a light-skinned Spaniard, told them rooms were 12.50 Pesos a night ($1.00 US). Charles, still buzzed and in a haze, was delighted. His second-floor room had a large bed, desk, chair, marble floor, windows to the street, and a complete bathroom with a tub. He could not have asked for more. This was indeed cool and, more importantly, more than reasonably priced. He put his suitcase on the bed and was about to say goodnight to Rod and the driver when it was "decided" they would go out on the town.

Back in the cab, the driver became their guide as they checked out several nightclubs and continued drinking. Charles cannot remember if he was paying for any of it because he had yet to change his dollars into pesos. As the first hints of dawn appeared, Rodrigo said it was enough partying for him, and they headed back to the hotel.

Having explained his goal to Rodrigo, mainly needing to connect with the recommended lawyer, he may have mentioned it to the driver. When they stopped at the hotel, the cabbie suggested (with a few phrases and sign language) that they could go for breakfast and later check out the lawyer.

Was it the alcohol? Charles did not hesitate about going with him. Without Rodrigo, it meant very little effective communication, but Charles managed to let the driver know it was OK with him. He remembers the breakfast vividly; his first plate of sunny-side eggs on delicious Mexican rice. Not having eaten for twelve hours, he might have welcomed anything. However, the pleasant memory of that breakfast has stayed with him over the years.

Charles showed the driver the lawyer's address and phone number, and the cabbie called for him, but there was no answer. They decided to drive to the office. Instead of an office, however, they arrived at an impressive home in an upscale neighborhood. Like many nearby houses, it had a metal bar pull-down grill covering the breezeway entrance. Behind the steel bars, which had a large mail slot, was a pile of dust-covered letters, periodicals, small packages, and newspapers. It appeared the house had been unoccupied for weeks. Regardless, they rang the front-door bell; there was no answer.

Charles did not react much to his disappointment. The driver, however, made some positive-sounding comments and motioned for Charles to get back into the cab. Not far from the upper-class neighborhood, they drove past ornate gates into what seemed to be a large park, with a historic palace-looking building on a hill above the roadway. The driver pulled off the main road, and they went by a group of men playing chess in the shade of several trees. They arrived at a small lake with rowboats for rent.

The driver signaled Charles an invitation to go for a boat ride and told him that this was Chapultepec Park. Several families and a few couples were in other boats, laughing and chattering away. Dance music was playing, but Charles could not tell where it came from. Now mid-morning, as the sun rose higher and higher, the *taxista* rowed Charles around the lake, apparently describing the park and its various attractions. Charles could not understand any of it.

* * *

To his utmost chagrin, besides the driver's name, Charles cannot remember if he paid the driver anything. Dropped off at the hotel, he never saw him again. Rodrigo was nonchalant about the post-arrival events when he got up around noon. Charles did not talk about them.

Not hungover and feeling refreshed after a three-hour nap, Charles was still in sustained disbelief. Only happenstance or guardian angels had him still in Mexico City. His urge to fly home had dissipated, but he was still anxious. He needed to find a lawyer and could not imagine how he could do it. He does not remember attempting to call the recommended lawyer again. The pile of debris inside the breezeway was all the information he needed. The Pasadena lawyer was not worth contacting either, given his misinformation. At least, that was how Charles saw it.

Rodrigo was only going to stay for two more days. When he left, Charles would have to navigate the city on his own. He decided that his first task was to find out how to contact Tam and where and how she could send him more funds. The thirty dollars would not last long. Rodrigo and the concierge helped make a person-to-person collect call to the US, which Tam refused, providing the first of many communication and money transfer problems. Charles called again without the person-to-person added costs, and she accepted the call. Repeating the information he received from the concierge and Rodrigo, he told her to wire money to the downtown Western Union office.

She was evasive about when she could send it, saying only that it would be soon. Charles reminded her that he not only needed enough money to live on but also to pay for the divorce. She said she would send more the next day. He considered mentioning the emptying of all their accounts, leaving him without a penny but chose not to do so. He wondered if she believed him when he said he had departed with only thirty of the hundred dollars, the rest spent on his plane tickets and other travel expenses. The folly of not asking for more money from her before he left or borrowing from his parents began to haunt him.

* * *

After talking to Tam about sending money, Rodrigo mentioned Maisie, and Charles returned to the present.

He had forgotten about their luncheon date and called the Hotel Bamer. She was still there and cheery as ever, recommending the Chalet Suizo restaurant in an upscale eatery and galleries district called the *Zona Rosa*. They agreed to meet there.

The concierge gave him a city map and showed him where it was. Charles decided to take a cab. Before he left, Rodrigo suggested they go out on the town after dinner, and Charles nodded yes.

Arriving at the Swiss restaurant not long after Maisie, he immediately felt out of place, convinced he was the shabbiest dressed patron. Then he realized that being an American tourist, he could probably wear almost anything. Besides, he was not inappropriately attired, wearing a sport shirt, khakis, and loafers. He calmed himself down and ordered veal stroganoff for the first time in his life.

Part of his mini-panic was Maisie. She was indeed as beautiful as he was incredulous that she would want his company. However, there she was, smiling and seemingly happy to tell him about her activities for the week. She invited him to join her on a noon tour of Bellas Artes the next day. Afterward, they could have a late lunch together. She had a voucher for the Hotel Mexico's rooftop restaurant overlooking the Zocalo.

He thanked her for the invitations, letting her know how much he appreciated them, besides giving him opportunities to explore the city with her. They ordered vanilla ice cream with Kahlua poured over it for dessert. The bitter taste in his mouth from speaking with Tam had all but disappeared.

Walking around the Zona Rosa, Maisie bought a few gifts she planned to take back to San Francisco. She commented on the quality of the window displays, providing him with multiple observations that he would have missed otherwise. It was a relaxing and enjoyable lunch and afternoon stroll, which helped Charles more than he realized. She suggested they meet at the Bellas Artes entrance around 11:30am. Charles agreed, thinking that he could also go to Western Union afterward.

Maisie was an enigma to him. He could not understand why she wanted him around. He was also gun-shy of rejection and avoided any situation that might lead to it, which might explain his reluctance to "approach" Maisie. He did like her company.

The last day and a half's whirlwind caught up with Charles upon return to the hotel. He took a nap but was not in the mood for a cantina tour after awakening. Rodrigo was also becoming fatigued, so they decided to go out for a beer and some snacks that Charles has never identified. He told Rodrigo a somewhat extended version of what had him in Mexico City. Rodrigo was philosophical and somewhat circumspect, perhaps having experienced something similar. The conversation turned to Maisie when Rodrigo asked if he had gone to bed with her. Charles laughed but felt a wave of anxiety. There was no chance he would take a step in that direction, kidding Rodrigo to mask his fears. Although feeling comfortable with Maisie, a gesture toward intimacy seemed too risky. He put her out of his mind and went to bed, getting up almost too late to meet at what looked like a massive, ornate marble palace.

Later, he learned its full name: *El Palacio de Bellas Artes*.

After a dazzling tour through Bellas Artes, Charles and Maisie walked down Avenida Cinco de Mayo towards the Zocalo and the Gran Hotel Ciudad de Mexico. Entering it, Charles was stunned; it had a multi-story atrium topped by a massive Tiffany-style curved stained glass ceiling-roof. With the midday sun providing vivid backlighting, it sparkled in a spellbinding kaleidoscope of colors. They stopped and gazed at it for several minutes without talking. Maisie mentioned it was "Art Nouveau" and took some photos.

The atrium and the fascinating stained-glass ceiling were examples of what Charles had begun to love about Mexico City—its artistic flare.

It was only his second day in the city, and everything seemed otherworldly to him. They took the elevator up to the rooftop restaurant, adding to his sense of unfamiliar luxury. The food was excellent, not expensive, and the view included the Basilica and the Presidential Palace, with a gigantic Mexican flag waving in the middle of the square.

Distracted from the purpose of his trip, Charles began to feel better.

"This is wonderful, but I need to get back to finding a lawyer soon. I'll talk to the concierge with Rodrigo translating tomorrow," he thought. Then, he changed his mind, deciding not to rush everything.

After the meal, he and Maisie visited the Basilica and the entrance to the Presidential Palace. Charles felt he was in a holy place inside the Basilica, which had an atmosphere unlike any Catholic church he had previously attended. Mass was in progress at a side altar, with small clouds of incense in the air. People were kneeling in the pews, praying, while others were shuffling the length of the cathedral's marble floor on their knees. It was a sanctuary of fervent devotional worship. American churches and parishioners now seemed cold and distant to him. These churchgoers were not just going through the motions; they expressed their beliefs in their prayers and actions. He felt humbled by their evident faith.

Walking back towards Bellas Artes, Charles mentioned he needed to see if there were any messages for him at Western Union. Maisie's hotel was a block or so past the office. She said she wanted to go into a bookstore to look for postcards and that it was next to Western Union.

Taking their time, they window-shopped and people-watched until San Juan de la Tran, the main north-south boulevard through the city's center. Charles had learned that crossing a street was sometimes risky, and crossing a wide boulevard was dangerous. Vehicles seemed to have the right of way in Mexico, not pedestrians. Even crossing with a green light did not guarantee you would not have to dodge a car, bus, or truck. The uncovered manholes in the sidewalks and other obstacles, and the risk of vehicle mayhem, made paying constant attention while walking mandatory. Charles liked it; there was a whiff of adventure while strolling along.

No money was waiting for him at Western Union. He was not surprised. He knew from bitter experience that Tam was not to be trusted.

"What if she never sends money?" he asked himself. "Then, what do I do?"

Charles imagined going to the US embassy and asking for help to return home. It seemed to him a possible solution, and he calmed down from his momentary panic.

Walking into the bookstore where Maisie looked over postcards helped because he was impressed with its artistic layout. Large picture windows faced Bellas Artes, while its interior sparkled with elegant and sophisticated displays of books, artwork, posters, and decorative plants. One more example of the artistry that was so common in the capital.

Having browsed, they headed toward Maisie's nearby hotel. Maisie asked Charles if he knew about the Diego Rivera mural in the Hotel del Prado, just past hers. He asked her if she wanted to see it, avoiding admitting he had no idea who Diego Rivera was.

"Yes, let's take a look at it; the guidebook says it is outstanding, and there is more information if you would like to read it while we are there," Maisie responded.

After Bellas Artes and the Gran Hotel de Ciudad de Mexico's "Art Nouveau" stained-glass ceiling, Charles began feeling enthusiastic about art. It was something he had never paid much attention to in the past. The mural, however, was a completely new experience.

Sitting down on a bench, they faced one of Rivera's masterpieces, *Sueño de una tarde dominical en la Alameda Central (Dream of a Sunday Afternoon in the Alameda Central[1])*. The mural covered a large wall, almost floor-to-ceiling and wall-to-wall. In its center stood Diego as a young boy, holding hands with a skeleton dressed elaborately in a florid European style popular with upper-class Mexican women. Called a *"Catrina,"* she also had a feathered serpent (*Quetzalcoatl*, a Pre-Columbian deity) around her neck, hanging down like a stole. Frida Kahlo, one of Rivera's wives and a brilliant artist, stood behind and between them, a symbol in one hand. Jose Guadalupe Posada, an artist and

---

1. *https://en.wikipedia.org/wiki/Alameda_Central*

printer, who Rivera saw as unappreciated and unrecognized, is to La Catrina's left.

The setting is around 1900 in the Alameda Central (a large park across the street from the del Prado and to one side of Bellas Artes). There are 150 figures in the painting: historical and present-day persons, rich and poor, heroes and villains, and the powerful and the weak. Charles had never seen anything like it; the panorama seemed to envelop him even without knowing most of the people in it.

Later, he learned the symbol in Kahlo's hand was the Yin-Yang, which conveys there is some spiritual in the physical and some physical in the spiritual, with a unifying circle around them.

(Note: Yin and Yang are literally the "dark side" and the "sunny side" of a hill. Chinese and other Eastern disciplines use this symbol to represent the opposites of the world's composition: dark and light, female and male, earth and heaven, death and birth, matter and spirit, and with a little of each other mixed in.)

According to the guidebook, the mural contains a variety of personages: some that were positive and some the opposite, some historical, some present-day, and a scattering of the Native poor.

Charles quickly realized that this painting would require serious study to glean as many nuances from it as possible. He decided to just feel it and not try to "understand" Rivera. He wondered if this was Rivera's vision of Mexican historical and present-day society.

After contemplating the mural, they explored the Alameda Central Park across the street. Founded in 1592, it is the oldest park in North America. With multiple fountains, tree-shaded promenades, playful children, and colorful vendors, the park seemed like a healing oasis in contrast with the heavy traffic noise and high-rises on both sides of it.

They sat down on one of the many benches and chatted. Things might have turned out differently if it had not been Charles' second day in the city. He liked being with Maisie, which seemed mutual, but she was well outside the realm of possibilities from his point of view.

Casually, Maisie asked him if he would like to see her hotel room.

"Sure," he responded, feeling slightly awkward. They walked out of the park and across Avenida Juarez to the Bamer. Considered a 4-star hotel, it had a somewhat modern elegance. Maisie's room on the fourteenth floor provided a panoramic vista of the Alameda, Bellas Artes, and the city for many miles.

Charles lingered for minutes at the window, transfixed by the view. Maisie stood in the center of the room, saying nothing. He told her it was a great hotel room, given its expansive views of the city's iconic landmarks. Seemingly relaxed but feeling uncomfortable, Charles kept his distance. He told her he had greatly enjoyed Bellas Artes, the rooftop lunch, Rivera's mural, and their walk in the park. About to thank her, she interrupted him and explained that she was going to Cuernavaca and Taxco for two days, and perhaps they could meet for lunch when she returned. He left after thanking her for a great second day in the city and that he would be delighted to meet for lunch when she returned.

Charles never saw her again.

* * *

Rodrigo was on the plane to Peru before Charles had learned much more than how to get to the Western Union office on foot. Maisie was gone before he knew it, telling him when he called that she had met some friends from San Francisco in Taxco and they would spend time together in the city. After that, Charles was alone and fearful. Tam had not sent money the next day as she promised, and his money was dwindling far too quickly. He called again; yes, money was on its way, which reminded him that Tam could look straight into your eyes without blinking and lie.

Charles guessed he would be in the city for three weeks or less. However, he had not imagined everything that could happen while he frustratingly attempted to secure the divorce. Nor had he considered his current state of (wounded) being, how hurt he was (cuckolded multiple times and then dumped), and, more importantly, how angry he was about almost everything that had happened during the last two years.

The availability of inexpensive alcohol—-a liter of dark Bacardi rum cost less than one dollar—was not helpful. His mental status, recent events, present circumstances, and *Cuba Libres* precipitated several threatening and dangerous episodes.

Almost a month into what seemed to Charles World War One trench warfare, he walked back to the hotel, inebriated, broke, frustrated (after another long, useless hike to Western Union), and with a non-existent fuse. Approaching a small marimba orchestra playing on a street corner, the music annoyed him. Convinced the musicians were laughing at him, he grabbed the marimba and tumbled it onto them. They careened backward like tenpins onto the concrete sidewalk while letting out a chorus of yells as it fell on them. Without breaking his stride, he continued to his hotel.

The following day he awoke with a sweaty start. Had that actually happened? Yes, it had. He was a familiar figure on his daily route; could the police already be in the hotel to arrest him?

Moving slowly to the stairwell, he peered down toward the concierge, who was pouring his ritual morning coffee extract and warm milk into what looked like a sundae glass, with an ever-present *pan dulce* sitting nearby in a white saucer. All was quiet.

Charles descended, nodded to him, and walked briskly down the same sidewalk from the night before. No one even gave him a threatening glance. Relieved, he continued his daily pilgrimage to the Western Union office, where money arrived sporadically. The concierge had helped him several times by giving him credit and lending him a few pesos.

The worst, however, was a week of severe illness, dysentery. Feverish and vomiting, with extreme diarrhea, and too weak to walk downstairs, he was critically ill. Worse yet, he would later realize, he had been drinking the same tap water that had made him sick in the first place.

When the maid arrived each morning, he would feebly wave to her for help.

She would snap, slamming the door, "*Borracho otra vez! Pinche gringo!*"

It wasn't until he recovered and spoke with a Mexican American in the hotel that he found out what she was saying.

"Drunk again! Stinking gringo!"

Recovering from dysentery without medication was more of a life-threatening ordeal than Charles realized. He knew he was sick, but the fever interfered with his ability to assess himself accurately. Near death for several days, only his youth, having "reserves" (fat) to burn, and staying in bed, saved him. Afterward, when he put on his pants, having lost so much weight, they fell straight to the floor without touching his waist or hips.

This life-threatening saga took place during the second week of his stay. With Rodrigo and Maisie gone, there was no one he could contact for help. Deep into the reality he feared upon arrival, he remembered his intense panic standing on the sidewalk outside the terminal. The only difference now was he had discovered he could be self-reliant. Fear was no longer as significant an issue.

Despite everything that had happened since his arrival, he had fallen in love with Mexico City. It was his first taste of being in an unknown society, culture, environment, and architecture. He loved it; everything was new, and even mundane activities were thrilling. The city's elegance overwhelmed him; department store window arrangements were, to him, works of art.

A year later, during a job-related physical exam, the doctor asked him, looking at his lab results, "Have you had any severe infections? Your blood has significant populations of germ-destroying cells."

Yes, he had developed antibodies and resistance during his stay...and quite a bit more.

* * *

Charles laughed ironically about his "*vacation* at their expense" idea. It had turned into a "Beyond Outward Bound" series of experiences. Broke, each day became a little worse. Then, he fell ill.

After his illness, the walk to the Western Union office felt like a twenty-mile slog with a heavy backpack. Fifty dollars were there; he could pay his mounting hotel bill and buy some food.

"Thank God for the concierge; without him, I'd be sleeping in doorways," he thought.

Chronically forlorn, he trudged back to the hotel. On the way, as he had in the past, he passed by the Hotel del Prado. Its front steps festooned with "guides" that annoyed him every time he walked by.

"Hey, Meester, want a young girl? No, a boy? Whatever you want, I get for you. What do you want?" was a familiar chorus.

That day, shuffling along and still weak a week later after his illness, Charles did something beyond any shadow of reason.

"What I want is a lawyer," he blurted to the exceptionally sleazy-looking pimp.

Taken aback, he looked Charles over, attempting to see if it was a joke or somehow in the realm of possibilities.

Charles said nothing and just stared at him.

"OK, Meester, I will take you to one," he said in a singsong fashion and motioned Charles to follow him.

Crossing San Juan de la Tran, they entered a district of old apartment, store, and office buildings, most four or five stories high. Charles had followed the unknown man without considering what he was doing. He was sick of the whole deal. If he got mugged or worse, that would end his ordeal. Fatalistically, he tagged along.

After a few blocks, they entered a nondescript building and took the elevator to the third floor. They faced a lettered door exiting the elevator, "Eduardo Calvo, Lic." Once inside, a secretary ushered them into a stately office.

Calvo sat behind an ornately carved wooden desk with a business-only expression on his face. The "guide" said a few quick words in Spanish that Charles could not understand.

Very professionally, in English, Calvo asked Charles a series of questions and then told him that he would have to fill out multiple forms and a questionnaire about why he wanted a divorce. He explained that the divorce would take about two weeks. Adding that recorded at both the US embassy here and the Mexican embassy in Los Angeles, California, it would be a legal divorce in both countries. His fee was $200.00 US.

Charles agreed on the spot.

He does not remember how much he gave the guide or if he gave him anything, perhaps leaving it up to Calvo. Deep in disbelief at how he had contacted this lawyer, he felt the same way about agreeing to have him do the divorce. The lawyer gave him the papers to fill out—thankfully, in English—and made an appointment for him to return.

It is going to happen, Charles stuttered to himself. But it seems unreal.

On the way to the hotel, he went into Sanborn's and had a light meal, not wanting to overburden his thoroughly weakened digestive tract. He managed to keep it down.

The next day, he called Tam and told her he had found a legitimate lawyer and that the divorce was underway. He needed the $200 post-haste and money to live on because it would take at least another two weeks. She agreed to send the money. Charles did not say anything; he did not care if she sent it or not. He was unsure if he wanted to return to California or stay in Mexico. He had reached a point that seemed uncomfortably foreign and utterly incomprehensible to him.

* * *

Charles' solo "Beyond Outward Bound" Mexico City saga lasted over six weeks. Multiple times over the years, he has marveled that he survived them.

Besides Moctezuma's Ultimate Revenge, several "not-one-stinkin'-peso-in-my-pocket" episodes were more than daunting. For Charles, it was not just being broke but not knowing if or when money would arrive. He did his best to enjoy the long walks, spending time in the Alameda along the way, gazing at the Rivera mural, or browsing in the nearby upscale bookstore. Finding nothing for him at Western Union much more often than not was painfully discouraging. He soon began repressing it, taking on a "What, me worry?" attitude. However, it was a sham. He did worry and became angry each time he walked back to the hotel empty-handed.

Predictably, the lawyer's fees were slow arriving, which added to his frustration because it appeared Calvo was dragging his heels until he received full payment. The best Charles could do at first was one hundred dollars. Communication with Tam was difficult, and often she did not answer the phone. The concierge was not delighted to have his telephone busy for as long as it took to set up a call, much less have it. Charles could feel the concierge's annoyance and worried he would suddenly decide to have him find another phone or, worse yet, another hotel.

Bacardi rum led to various situations that Charles realized later were definitely dangerous. With cognitive functions out the window, he did not have a care in the world. Not long after Rodrigo and Maisie were gone, he made friends with a Mexican-American, Valentin, in the hotel. Valentin had lost an eye in an industrial accident in the US and received monthly compensation, but it was only enough to live on in Mexico. He had an attractive girlfriend, Gloria, who was blonde, full-bodied, and seemed reserved and circumspect to Charles. She only spoke Spanish, which made communication with her almost impossible.

Valentin turned out to be somewhat of a leech. He lent Charles money at first but later asked Charles to lend him some. Little by little, the balance sheet leaned toward Valentin owing Charles, but that was OK because when he was broke, Valentin had helped. Not long into their friendship, they began to play cards, but not for money. At times without funds, Charles enjoyed the distraction of the card games. Besides that, Valentin would translate for Charles when necessary.

Once their friendship was established, Valentin let Charles know that he was Gloria's "guide" and that she was available for more than cards. Feeling foolish at being so naïve, Charles ignored the message. It seemed bizarre to him to be friends with Valentin and have sex with Gloria. In particular, because they all lived in the same hotel and Gloria had a six-year-old son who was with them or just visited. Charles never figured out that part.

The lawyer paid and the divorce in progress; Charles had time on his hands. Finally, he had some money, about one hundred dollars. The delay in paying Calvo had pushed back the divorce completion a week or so. Charles planned to leave the day after the filing, which had yet to be established. Now, his walks to Western Union were instead to Calvo's office to find out the divorce's status. Calvo was straightforward with Charles; he had to get the divorce in Cuernavaca, where a friend was a judge. It would not diminish its legality, but it would take longer. He stated that he was doing everything to move the divorce toward completion.

Charles felt he was back to square one. Was Calvo taking him for the proverbial ride? Was he stringing him along and then would ask for more money? Worst of all, the divorce might never be finalized. Calvo had seemed so professional and sincere to Charles. A front? He did his best to suppress his worries. The saying goes, "in for a penny, in for a pound," but Charles was in for two thousand five hundred pesos.

* * *

Eight dollars, a hundred pesos, covered eight days' rent at the San Cosme. It was what Charles would have paid for a night with Gloria. He avoided Valentin's suggestion, and it would lead to a near-death experience. Valentin had a few male friends, tough-looking types, in and out of the hotel. They seemed to relate to Valentin and Gloria as a couple. That Valentin had suggested the "pinche" gringo spend the night with Gloria did not go down well. Charles' refusal, it seemed, made it even worse. He noticed it in their faces and body language. Now, they mad-dogged him when before they had been coolly friendly. Valentin seemed oblivious to it all. Later, Charles wondered what he was up to, no doubt knowing his friends' reaction in advance. Even Gloria developed a hostile attitude toward him.

None of this would have been an issue, but there was a party in someone's home, and Charles attended with Valentin, Gloria, and their friends. After mucho Bacardi and Tequila, one of the male friends picked a fight with Charles, a knife in his hand. It ended as soon as it started, and Charles sobered up enough to realize he was in a dangerous situation, as there was no easy exit. They were on the second story, and Valentin's "friends" were between him and the stairway.

Unexpectedly, an American (Charles had not realized he was a compatriot), speaking fluent Spanish, intervened and calmed everyone down. A little later, he introduced himself and talked with Charles, saying he was a student at Mexico City College, a US-accredited college with extraterritorial status. Through the choppy sea of Bacardi and adrenaline, Charles filed the information away in the back of his mind. It would later become significant.

Everyone acted as if nothing had happened the next day at the hotel. Charles finally learned a lesson, though, no more Bacardi-fueled outings. This was the stretch run; the divorce was supposedly about to be finalized. He was ready to return to "boring" California and register for the next semester at Pasadena City College.

* * *

He did not kiss the ground when the plane landed in Tijuana, but he felt like doing so. His six-week-plus boot camp was over, and so was the divorce, now filed in both countries. Calvo had done his job professionally and efficiently. From time to time, remembering how he found Calvo, Charles chalked it up to another guardian angel episode; he could not think of any other explanation.

The TJ flight was grueling.

One of the Connie's engines had bronchitis on the tarmac, and everyone had to disembark. After an hour or more wait, they climbed onto a smaller plane, a two-motor. Charles did not recognize its make or pedigree. It was much slower than the Constellation and arrived much later than expected, resulting in multiple delays to reach LA by bus.

Arriving long after midnight, he decided not to call his parents. Even at that hour, there were many individuals in the station. With no bus to Pasadena scheduled until the morning, he called out, "Anyone going to Pasadena?" Almost immediately, he received a ride offer. The angels were still around.

After his return, he spoke very little about his Mexico City experiences. His marriage and the way it ended hurt for years.

* * *

Not long after Charles came back, a major earthquake struck Mexico City. The *Angel de la Independencia,* a massive golden statue revered by *"Chilangos"* (Mexico City residents), fell from its tall pillar and shattered.

Standing high above one of the many Paseo de la Reforma *glorietas* (traffic circles), it was a revered landmark. Shrine-like to many Mexicans, Charles walked by it multiple times, impressed with its splendor, shining brightly in the middle of the Paseo de la Reforma.

The earthquake and the fall of El Angel reminded Charles of a somewhat eerie experience he had while walking along "Reforma." He noticed a mob congregated down a side street. Hundreds, if not thousands of Mexicans, were lined up and crowding toward a building in the middle of the block. He asked a passerby about it.

"Se murio Pedro Infante," he told Charles, choking up. Pedro Infante had died.

The crowds were outside the funeral home, where Infante lay in a closed coffin.

Charles did not know who Infante was but said he was sorry in Spanish. Later, he learned that Infante was one of Mexico's biggest stars. Valentin explained the enormity of the loss, detailing his many talents and that he was at the peak of his career. It sounded as if Frank Sinatra had died prematurely. Infante perished in a plane crash and burned so severely that a gold bracelet and a metal plate in his forehead (from a previous plane crash!) were the only means to identify him.

* * *

A massively destructive earthquake in 1985 devastated Mexico City. The Hotel Bamer survived, but the del Prado collapsed. Luckily, Rivera's mural had only minor damage.

After a successful public campaign to save the mural, removing it from the shattered hotel became the next hurdle. To do so, they cut the wall from the building and assembled a metal structure around it to support its 15-ton weight. Lifted by crane and transported carefully to a nearby site, a museum and its facilities were built around it.

The *Museo Mural Diego Rivera* opened on February 19, 1988.

The Hotel Bamer closed its doors in 2006, and the building sold. It remained empty for years and ultimately designated a historical landmark.

* * *

Two years after coming back to the United States, Charles returned to Mexico City, having enrolled in Mexico City College.

The Founders of Mexico City College

Dr. Paul V. Murray

Dr. Paul V. Murray, born June 15, 1908, Chicago, IL, "His contributions to the local Mexican-English community have been wide and varied. He was a founding member and the first American vice president of the Mexican-American Institute of Cultural Relations; a founding member of the American Society; secretary of the organizing committee that founded Colegio Tepeyac and Colegio Guadalupe; a member of the organizing committee that founded St. Patrick's Church, now the Anglo-American parish in Mexico City; and a founding member of the committee that established Junípero Serra School.

"He started teaching at the American High School in August 1936, became Principal in September 1939, and resigned from the High School in July 1, 1946, the year MCC moved into its own buildings and he became Dean and Vice-Principal of Mexico City College. Dr, Murray aided in planning the buildings and grounds of the American School in Tacubaya, and he helped to promote the spread of American football, basketball, and softball in connection with his work at MCC and at the American School." Murray received his honorary Doctor of Law degree from his alma mater. In 1958, Dr. Murray was selected as the recipient of the Twenty-Fifth Catholic Action medal given by

St. Bonaventure University. He is listed in *Who's Who in American Education, Leaders in American Education, International Who's Who, and American Catholic Who's Who.* He has written widely in the fields of education, Mexican history, and contemporary affairs." Murray wrote <u>The Catholic Church in Mexico: 1519-1920</u>, and privately published in 1965. He started but never finished the second volume. Dr. Murray died November 4, 1984, in Mexico City. Cremated, his remains are in La Iglesia de Covadonga in Colonia Palmas, along with his wife, Elena Picazo de Murray.

When the Universidad de las Americas, Puebla, named a building after Dr. Murray and Dr. Cain, the school invited Dr. Murray's son, Paul V. Murray, Jr., Ph.D., and his two sisters, all expenses paid, as guests to the Dedication (March 1, 1998).

As Paul Murray, Jr. wrote, "The Inauguration was truly a supreme and far-reaching gesture by UDLAP in recognition of its heritage (that) honored my father's (and Dr. Cain's) vision."

(Adapted from the MCC Collegian, Vol. 20, October 18, 1956, and private correspondence.)

MCC 1940's DF entrance.

Dr. Henry L. Cain

In 1944, with the help of Dr. Paul V. Murray, Cain planned the new American School located, with a limited enrollment of 1,500 students, on a 125-acre plot in Tacubaya, donated by old-time colony resident S. Bolling Wright. Wright became President of the School Board. To accommodate the overflow of the American School, Dr. Cain founded and built Colegio Columbia, located across from the present American School. Colegio Columbia, founded in 1938 to teach English to non-English speaking students, opened in the building erected by Dr. Cain at San Louis Potosí, where the Clases de Inglés and Clases Comerciales now operate. Elena Picazo de Murray, wife of Dr. Paul V. Murray, was instrumental in developing the English classes.

"In 1940, Drs. Cain and Murray founded Mexico City College to further education for the graduates of the American High School and to make a center for continuous study for visiting Americans. It was in the American High School building until 1946. Cain served as first President until June 11, 1953, when Dr. Murray became President.

"Cain was the Potentate of the Shriners when Mexico's ex-President Miguel Alemán entered the local chapter in 1944. Cain led the campaign to get the North American Shriners to establish in Mexico what was their sixteenth hospital for crippled children. He became Vice Chairman of the Board of

Directors of the Mexican hospital that today (1957) has 30 beds and performs 200 operations on poor crippled children of Mexico."

When the Universidad de las Americas, Puebla, named a building after Dr. Murray and Dr. Cain, the school invited Dr. Murray's son, Paul V. Murray, Jr., Ph.D., and his two sisters, all expenses paid, as guests to the Dedication (March 1, 1998).

As Paul Murray, Jr. wrote, "The Inauguration was truly a supreme and far-reaching gesture by UDLAP in recognition of its heritage (that) honored my father's (and Dr. Cain's) vision."

(Adapted from the MCC Collegian, Vol. 20, October 18, 1956, and private correspondence.)

Joseph Murray Quinn

Obituary

Joseph Murray Quinn passed away at his Independence residence on December 29, 2018 at the age of 88. He was born January 22, 1930, Baton Rouge, LA to Issac Odom Quinn and Charlotte Dorsey of Bogalusa, LA. From age 3, he was raised in Long Beach, CA by his grandparents, Charlotte and Mayrant Dorsey, also formerly of Bogalusa, LA. He graduated from Woodard Wilson High School, and attended Long Beach City College. In Southern California he was an ardent swimmer and surfer, an active Boy Scout and cyclist.

Quinn served in the US Navy during the Korean Conflict, stationed in Japan and on an aircraft carrier with the Attack Squadron 125. Following the Navy, he worked under civilian contract in the Marshall Islands, South Pacific.

His undergraduate work was at Mexico City College (now, the Universidad de las Americas, Puebla, and UDLA A.C.), where he received his B.A. in Art, minor in Archaeology, in 1959. During his three and half years in Mexico, he lived in a small village, (Cuajimalpa) in the mountains above Mexico City.

Quinn lived in Spokane, WA from 1960 to 1968 before attending Washington State University. He received his Master's Degree from the School of Speech and Communications, Department of Theatre, WSU, Pullman, WA in 1970.

Much of Quinn's career has been in art, primarily theatre. He taught Theatre Arts at O.S.U and the University of Portland, and summer workshops at Spokane Community College and Holly Names Academy. He has designed stage scenery for, among many others, Gonzaga University, the Seattle Opera Association, and lighting for the Portland Opera Association, and scenery for the State Ballet of Oregon. He served as Designer and Technical Director for the Spokane Concert Ballet Productions.

Quinn was the founding-director for the Oakland Gaslight Players, Inc., the Umpqua Valley Community Theatre (UACT), Inc. (Roseburg, OR), founder and Artistic Director of Northwest Arena Theatre, Inc. (later becoming the NW Actors Theatre, Inc., (Spokane, WA). He served as Trustee with the Theatre Northwest, Inc., (a University of Washington playwriting group), and on the Douglas County Planning Committee (Oregon) for the State-wide Exp '86 booth in Vancouver, B.C. He was co-owner of the Oakland Studio of Ballet, and sponsored and toured 14 out-of-state ballet companies into Oregon.

After working on it for ten years, Quinn created a website in 2006 for the history he wrote about his alma mater, *The Mexico City College Story*: https://mexicocitycollege.com/ He transferred it to a fellow alumnus, Jed Linde, in 2016, who converted it into a book in 2024. https://books2read.com/u/mvPQj6

Quinn, along with a co-worker, surveyed the historical homes in Oakland, OR, resulting in this town designated as the first Historical District in Oregon.

Throughout his career, Quinn's artistic endeavors included painting, working in oils, acrylics, and watercolor and silk screening and woodcarving (baroque scrolls style).

Quinn is survived by his daughter, Tami Fox, two grandchildren, Kasey and Krystal, one great-grandson, Camden, and his loving companion of thirty years, Sheila T. Nelson.